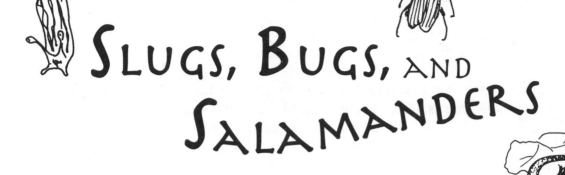

Slugs, Bugs, and Salamanders

Discovering Animals in Your Garden

Sally Kneidel

Illustrated by Anna-Maria Crum

fulcrum kids
Golden, Colorado

Text copyright © 1997 Sally Stenhouse Kneidel
Illustrations © 1997 Anna-Maria Crum

Book design by Alyssa Pumphrey

Library of Congress Cataloging-in-Publication Data
Kneidel, Sally Stenhouse.
    Slugs, bugs, and salamanders : discovering animals in your garden / Sally Stenhouse Kneidel ; illustrated by Anna-Maria Crum.
        p.   cm.
    Includes index.
    Summary: Focuses on the insects, birds, amphibians, and other animal life found in gardens, including creatures both beneficial and damaging, and discusses the best ways to care for garden plants.
    ISBN 1-55591-313-x (Pbk.)
    1. Garden ecology—Juvenile literature. 2. Garden animals—Juvenile literature. 3. Garden ecology—Study and teaching—Activity programs—Juvenile literature. 4. Gardening—Juvenile literature.
[1. Garden animals. 2. Garden ecology. 3. Gardening. 4. Ecology.] I. Crum, Anna-Maria, ill. II. Title.
    QH541.5.G37K54   1997
    577.5′54—dc21   96-48161
                                                                      CIP
                                                                      AC

Printed in the United States of America
0 9 8 7 6 5 4 3 2 1
Fulcrum Publishing
350 Indiana Street, Suite 350
Golden, Colorado 80401-5093
(800) 992-2908 • (303) 277-1623

TABLE OF CONTENTS

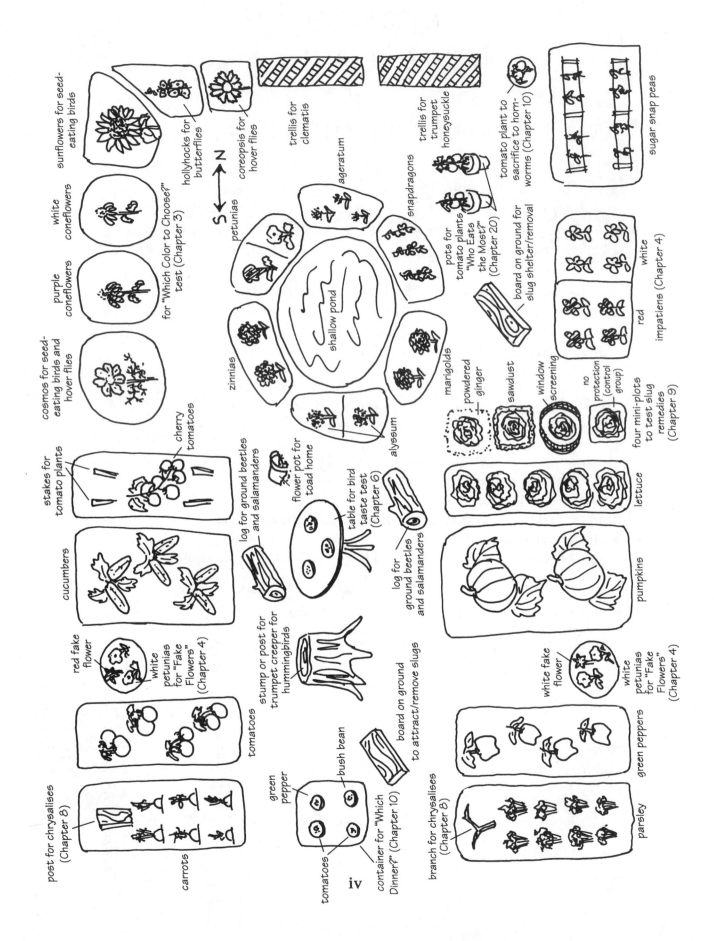

sunflowers for seed-eating birds

hollyhocks for butterflies

coreopsis for hover flies

trellis for clematis

trellis for trumpet honeysuckle

tomato plant to sacrifice to hornworms (Chapter 10)

sugar snap peas

white coneflowers

for "Which Color to Choose?" test (Chapter 3)

purple coneflowers

N

S

petunias

ageratum

snapdragons

pots for tomato plants "Who Eats the Most?" (Chapter 20)

board on ground for slug shelter/removal

red   white

impatiens (Chapter 4)

cosmos for seed-eating birds and hover flies

zinnias

shallow pond

marigolds

powdered ginger

sawdust

window screening

no protection (control group)

four mini-plots to test slug remedies (Chapter 9)

cherry tomatoes

alyssum

stakes for tomato plants

log for ground beetles and salamanders

flower pot for toad home

table for bird taste test (Chapter 6)

log for ground beetles and salamanders

lettuce

cucumbers

pumpkins

red fake flower

white petunias for "Fake Flowers" (Chapter 4)

stump or post for trumpet creeper for hummingbirds

board on ground to attract/remove slugs

white fake flower

white petunias for "Fake Flowers" (Chapter 4)

post for chrysalises (Chapter 8)

tomatoes

green pepper

bush bean

container for "Which Dinner?" (Chapter 10)

tomatoes

branch for chrysalises (Chapter 8)

green peppers

parsley

carrots

iv

Introduction

What Kind of Garden Is This About?

This book describes a garden especially for children. In this garden are playful vegetables that seem designed for children, like cherry tomatoes and sugar peas that you can pop in your mouth right off the vine! This garden has flowers that are fun too—snapdragons that bite the air when you pinch them and sunflowers for munching.

But this is a garden not just of plants. It's an animal garden too! All gardens are shared by animals, and with this book you'll learn the different roles they play. You'll learn how to attract the ones that are beautiful, how to make homes for the ones that are helpful, and how to discourage those that are pests.

The Plants and the Garden Community

Plants have no mouths. They don't eat. They make their own food inside their bodies using the energy of the sun. You can't do that. If you wcrc to put your feet in the garden soil, stretch out your arms, and let the sun shine on you for weeks, you wouldn't be making food. You'd just be getting sunburned and very hungry.

Humans and animals don't have the ability to produce food using sunlight. So we have to eat the plants' food, which is stored in the plants. Or we can eat other animals that have eaten the plants.

Every community of living things, like a desert community or a woodland community or a human community, must have plants. Without them, everything else in the community will starve.

So the plants are the most important part of your garden. They support everything else.

Some of the plants in this garden make flowers for butterflies and hummingbirds. Some make seeds for songbirds. And some of the plants in this garden make vegetables, not only for you, but for the small friends you'll be observing.

Producers and Consumers

Because plants alone are able to produce food with their own bodies, they are called nature's "producers." Because animals consume food instead of producing it, they are called "consumers."

A "primary consumer" is an animal that eats plants. "Primary consumer" means first consumer. They're first in line after the producers. Aphids, slugs, rabbits, and cows are primary consumers.

An animal that eats a primary consumer is a "secondary consumer." If you eat beef, you are a secondary consumer. A fox that eats a rabbit is a secondary consumer. Can you name some of the secondary consumers in this book? (Look at the titles of Chapters 11 through 20.)

Are you also a primary consumer?

The Plant-Eaters

A plant-eater, or herbivore, is an animal that eats any part of a plant. This doesn't necessarily damage the plant, just as it doesn't damage you to have your hair or nails cut. In fact some plant parts, like fruits and nectar, are meant to be eaten. When fruits are eaten by animals, the seeds of the fruit get spread out to new places where they might grow.

Four of the plant-eaters featured in this book—the butterflies, hummingbirds, hover flies, and songbirds—are not harmful to plants. The butterflies, hummingbirds, and hover flies eat only the nectar of flowers. Nectar is a sugary liquid that is just for eating. If you've ever eaten the drop of sweet liquid in a honeysuckle flower, then you've eaten nectar. The flower trades its nectar for the powdery yellow pollen that the bees and butterflies bring from other flowers. The plant needs the pollen in order to form seeds and fruits. (All the flowers in Chapters 3, 4, and 5 were chosen for this garden because they produce a lot of nectar.)

The goldfinches and songbirds in Chapter 6 eat seeds. Although seed-eating birds don't help a plant, they don't hurt it either. The flowers in this garden that were chosen for their seeds—the sunflowers, zinnias, cosmos—make many more seeds than they need in order to replace themselves. They have plenty to spare.

Unlike birds and butterflies, many plant-eaters *do* damage plants. You'll meet five of these plant-damaging plant-eaters in Chapters 7 through 10, along with some of the vegetables they pester. The first villain is the aphid, a tiny herbivore that eats only the sap of plants. The tiny holes the aphids poke to suck the sap are too small to see. A few aphids on a plant will do no damage at all. But large numbers of aphids on one plant can drain so much sap that the plant wilts and dies. The "Aphid Babies Game" in Chapter 7 will show you how quickly an aphid population can get big enough to hurt your pumpkins, cucumbers, sugar peas, lettuce, and tomatoes.

In Chapter 8 you'll meet caterpillars, plant-eaters that focus on leaves. The black swallowtail caterpillars featured in this chapter eat the leaves of carrot and parsley plants. These particular caterpillars just take portions of the leaf, not enough to kill the plant or even affect its growth very much. When grown, the caterpillars will metamorphose into big beautiful butterflies right in the garden. A butterfly that has just emerged from the chrysalis may agree to cling to your finger as it dries and straightens its wings.

Chapters 9 and 10 describe the pesky slugs, snails, and hornworms and some of the plants you'll have to rescue from them. These irksome but interesting creatures devour both leaves and fruits, such as tomatoes.

The Predators That Eat the Plant-Eaters

The predators in Chapters 11 through 20 are all animals that eat the troublesome plant-eaters. So they are the gardener's friends. The predatory helpers in this book are ground beetles, lizards, salamanders, toads, mantises, crab spiders, worm snakes, box turtles, assassin bugs, and braconid wasps.

Each of these ten chapters describes one particular predator and the prey it eats. You'll be making little homes for some of these predators, and some homes will need to be near the vegetables. That's where the prey will be. The "Garden Map" on page iv shows where you might place these homes. You can learn to hand-feed some of the predators.

The Decomposers

The living things that eat and break down dead plants and animals are called "decomposers." Without them, fallen trees, dead elephants, and all dead things would lie where they fall forever. And we would quickly run out of space on our planet. But instead the decomposers chew up the dead plants and animals and turn them into soil, which is something we've got to have. Soil provides minerals that plants need, and it provides an anchor for their roots. In Chapter 21 you'll learn how to make a worm hotel. You can see how worms turn kitchen scraps into soil.

Which one of the creatures in this book will you like the best? The plant stabbers, the fairylike butterflies, the slimy worms and slugs, or the ones who eat the others alive? Meet them all and see.

A GARDEN JOURNAL

Keeping a garden journal can be fun and useful. A spiral notebook is good enough. You can write down what you planted, when, and where. Make a map of your garden in the journal. If it turns out that you planted too early and some seedlings got caught in a frost, then next year you can time things differently. It's useful too to write down how long it took each seed type to sprout. That will help you next year in knowing how long to leave the plastic sheet over the seeds. How long did it take before the lettuce shot into flower? Writing down the dates of all the major garden events—planting, sprouting, flowering, harvest, and uprooting—will help you in future planning.

A journal will also help you remember the joyful moments of gardening. I make note of any interesting animals I see, what they were doing, and the date. On what day did I see the first wasp cocoons on the hornworms? On what day did I see the first adult mantis? They often show up on almost the same date in later years. So I know when to start looking for them.

Another reason to keep a garden journal is to record the results of the experiments in this book. You probably won't remember numbers and details later if you don't write them down. You may have ideas about doing the experiments a little differently next year. Or you may want to use your results for next winter's science project.

The main reason for keeping a garden journal is that it's fun to look back through it later.

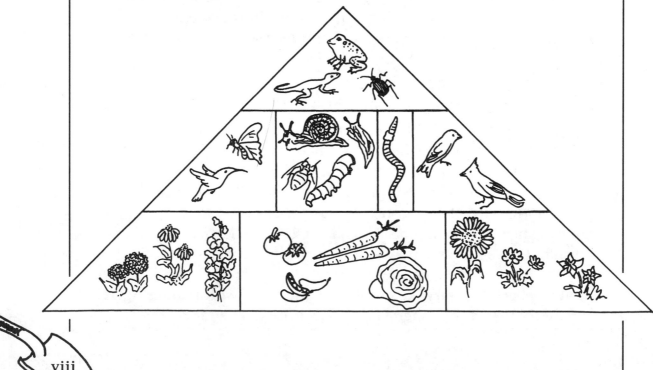

THE PLANTS

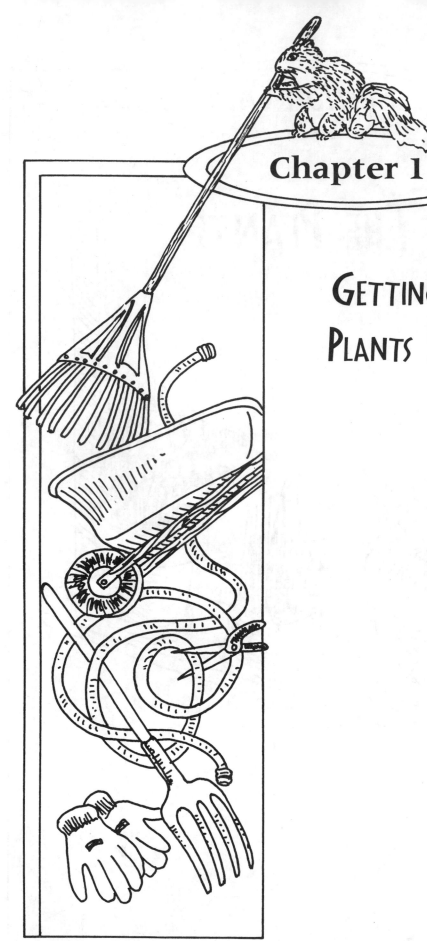

Chapter 1

GETTING YOUR PLANTS STARTED

Black Dirt Under Your Fingernails

Gardening is a good excuse to get your hands and knees really dirty. The soil is where it all starts for a gardener, on a warm spring day. The soil even smells good on such a day, an earthy outdoor smell. The best soil is the kind that will get you the very dirtiest—loose, moist, dark brown soil, with tiny bits of dead plants in it. And A LOT of worms.

Some soils need help getting to that smells-good dirty-knees state. If your soil is very sandy or breaks into very hard chunks when you try to dig in it, you may need to add some decomposed (rotting) plant matter to it. (You can provide your own decomposed plant matter by composting all your dead leaves and vegetable scraps, and adding them to the garden the following spring.) If your soil needs help now, you can buy decomposed animal manure in bags at a garden store. It works well too.

The soil in a garden needs to be loosened before seeds or new plants are planted. Soil for a small garden can be loosened with a shovel. Sounds like work, but if your soil is good, you're sure to find some wiggly worms and fat white grubs (beetle larvae) along the way. Your parents might rent a tiller from a hardware store to loosen soil for a larger garden. A tiller is hard to handle—let your parents do it.

Most of the plants recommended here need full sun for at least six hours each day. They may survive with less but will probably not bloom or produce vegetables. The lettuce and carrots can get by with perhaps five hours.

COMPOSTING

Composting is a way of recycling old plants, leaves, or vegetable matter that you don't need anymore. If you pile up these old plant parts, keep them wet, and let them sit for several months, they'll turn into very rich healthy soil that you can put back in your garden. Some people buy or build compost containers. A compost bin may be just a simple wood frame with chicken-wire sides. Others are plastic. All must have spaces for air to circulate. But you don't have to have a container to compost. I found a spot in my backyard that works fine. It's a space about five feet wide, between my back fence and my garden shed. In autumn I put all the dead raked leaves there. All the grass clippings go there too. (If your parents put any chemicals on your lawn to kill weeds or insects, then don't add grass clippings to your compost.) Any kind of yard waste, such as twigs that have been trimmed from shrubs, can go there.

You can compost not only yard and garden waste but also kitchen waste. My family keeps a compost bucket by the kitchen sink, lined with a plastic grocery bag. All of our kitchen scraps, except meat and eggs, go in the compost bucket. This includes table scraps, peelings, coffee grounds, moldy fruits or vegetables, eggshells, as well as wood ashes. The bucket gets full about every three or four days. Then we take it outside. We use a pitchfork to dig a hole in the big compost pile (which is mostly leaves). After we dump the vegetable stuff in the hole, we use the pitchfork to cover it back up completely. If it's not covered completely and at least a foot deep, then wild animals may smell it and dig it out.

Weeds from the garden can be composted, but sometimes the weed seeds will survive. Then they can grow new weeds when you put the compost back in the garden.

Leave out charcoal ashes, which may have bad chemicals. Leave out any animal products, which can attract rats. Leave out any plant parts that have been sprayed with bug sprays or weed sprays. Tomato diseases can be spread to next year's plants through compost, so don't compost tomatoes or tomato plants.

The compost pile must be kept moist. You may want to hose it down every week or so. I rarely hose mine, but I live in a place where it rains a lot. Deep inside the compost pile, bacteria go to work on the plant matter, eating it and breaking it down. The chemical reactions of the bacteria give off heat so that the center of the pile gets quite warm. If you turn the pile with a pitchfork on a cold day, steam will come off the center of it. Over a few months, most of the plant matter is gradually turned into soil.

Some gardeners turn their piles over with a pitchfork as often as every week. This gives every part of it a turn at the warm center, where the bacterial action is. Some turn it every few months. I seldom turn mine, so only the stuff on the bottom decomposes. Every January we push the past autumn's leaves to the back of the pile, out of the way. Then we dig up the rest—the new black rich soil—which is just over a year old. We drag it on a tarp to the garden and mix it with the soil that's already there. There are a few pieces of leaves still in it, ones that haven't decomposed completely, but that's okay. When we're through mixing, the garden soil looks black. It feels spongy and rich to our bare feet. It smells like spring. We're ready for planting!

WHERE TO PLANT YOUR FLOWERS AND VEGETABLES

The "Garden Map" on page iv shows one possible arrangement for your garden. If you change it, there are a few guidelines you should still keep in mind.

1. More butterflies will come to the flowers in Chapter 1 if the flowers are sheltered somewhat from the wind. A low area is less windy than a hilltop.
2. Sunflowers, trellises for hummingbird flowers, sugar peas, and anything else very tall should go on the north end of your garden to avoid blocking the sunlight to the other plants.
3. All the flowers selected to produce nectar or seeds for birds (Chapters 4 and 6) should be placed well away from shrubs or other possible hiding places for cats.

4. Homes or hiding places for toads, salamanders, and ground beetles (predators) should probably not be next to your carrots and parsley if you want the butterfly caterpillars that eat these plants to live for experimental purposes.

WHEN TO PLANT

For the flowers, tomatoes, cucumbers, beans, and pumpkins, wait until all danger of frost has passed before planting. This is usually between April 15 and May 15, depending on how far north you live. (Ask at the store where you buy them.) Carrots, lettuce, and sugar peas are cool-weather plants and should be set out one month earlier than the others.

STARTING THE GARDEN WITH YOUNG PLANTS

Most of the plants in the book can be purchased as baby plants (called bedding plants) in hardware stores or plant nurseries in the spring or early summer. They dry out very quickly in the little plastic store containers, so plant them right away or water them frequently.

Before taking your little plants out of the containers, decide on the placement of each one. The plants should come with a plastic tag that has planting instructions, including how far apart to put them. If not, think about the size of the adult plants when spacing the young ones. The grown plants should not be touching.

Make a little hole in the soil for each plant, the same size as the root and soil mass.

Water the plant immediately before taking it out of the pot. This causes the soil to stick to the roots, which protects them. Roots shouldn't be exposed to air if possible.

Run a plastic knife (not a sharp one) around the edge of the soil mass, between the soil and the inside of the pot. This loosens the soil from the pot, so it will all come out with the roots in one big chunk. You can probably pull the plant gently from the pot then by grasping the stem at the base, right next to the soil. If not, twist the plastic pot, as you would twist an ice tray, to loosen the plants more.

After you put the plants in the holes, firm the soil around them. They should be watered immediately after planting to fill any air pockets underground.

PLANTING SEEDS INSTEAD

Some plants grow easily from seed. A pack of seeds will give you more plants for your money than buying already-started plants. Individual chapters will tell you if the plants in that chapter will grow easily from seed. Some seeds, like those of impatiens flowers, are so small that they are hard to get started outside. If you want to, you can start very small seeds in pots indoors. The plants can be moved into the ground when they're a few inches tall. If you do that, follow the instructions in the section above for setting them into the ground.

Seed packages should tell you how deep to plant the seeds and how far apart to plant them. In general, you can plant seeds closer together than you would young plants. That's because not all the seeds will come up. If they come up too close to each other, you can just pull up the ones that look least healthy (a process called "thinning") and toss them on the compost pile.

Some gardeners plant their seeds in mounds of soil, or long thin parallel piles of soil, called rows. I think one reason they do that is to make the soil deeper just under the seeds. Maybe having the plants in rows makes it easier for the gardener to move around. But I just scatter my seeds at random in the plot I've chosen for them. Each gardener has his or her own style.

In general most seeds need about 1/4 inch of soil thrown over them. This doesn't have to be exact. Big seeds, like pumpkin seeds and bean seeds, can be planted about an inch deep. Snapdragons and alyssum should be just pressed lightly into the surface. If the information on the seed packet differs from the advice in this book, do what the seed packet says. Your seeds may be a different variety.

After you've planted, water the seeds gently with a sprinkler or a nozzle set on a gentle spray. A heavy stream from a hose may wash the seeds away.

CONTAINER GARDENS

If you live in an apartment building, you may want to have a container garden. You can grow vegetables and flowers in flower pots on indoor windowsills! You can grow them in barrels, buckets, or big pots on patios or balconies.

Tall vegetables and flowers, heavy vegetables, and those that climb will be easier to manage in large containers (5 or 10 gallons) on the patio or rooftop, rather than on windowsills.

But windowsills will work for all leafy vegetables, radishes, small varieties of tomatoes (pixie or Tiny Tim), small varieties of carrots (Nantes shorts or little finger), beets, and most herbs and flowers. An 8-inch pot is big enough.

Scatter seeds in each pot, then thin later. Thin carrots to 1 or 2 inches apart, radishes to 1 inch apart. Beans and peas should be 20 inches apart; melons, 6 inches apart. Thin lettuce plants to 8 inches apart, which means only one grown plant in an 8-inch pot. You can eat young lettuce plants that you remove while thinning. Thin flowers and other vegetables according to the package, or use your own judgment. You may want to plant them a little closer together in a container to make the most out of your space.

Light is a major concern when growing plants in containers. Vegetables that produce fruits (tomatoes, cucumbers, pumpkins) will need six hours of direct sun a day. This means they will probably need to be on a patio or in a window that faces south or west. Most flowers need six full hours a day too, except impatiens. In a window facing east, or a patio, you can grow leafy vegetables (like lettuce) and root vegetables (carrots, beets), but not fruits like tomatoes or pumpkins. A northern-facing space gets the least light. But you may still be able to grow lettuce and radishes.

If you don't have flower pots, you can try growing vegetables and flowers in anything—an old wagon; a 3-liter pop bottle cut in half; a wooden box; a bushel basket or wicker basket lined with plastic; an old kettle, can, or fishbowl; an old toy dump truck. In general, taller plants will need deeper containers. Otherwise, their roots will not be able to anchor them, and they'll fall over. So if you have only shallow containers, choose short plants.

When deciding whether to water, poke your finger all the way down into the soil. Do this on the edge so you won't damage roots. If you feel no moisture two or three inches down, or if your plant is wilting, then water. Don't water every day. When you do water, try to moisten the soil all the way down.

Most plants do better if the container has drainage holes in the bottom, so extra water can get out. You don't want too much extra water though. Water carries nutrients away. If your containers do have holes, be sure to put pans under them indoors to catch the dribble. If your containers have no holes, be careful not to water too much. Sitting in a pool of water is not good for roots. Sound complicated? You'll get the hang of it.

Good luck! You're under way!

9

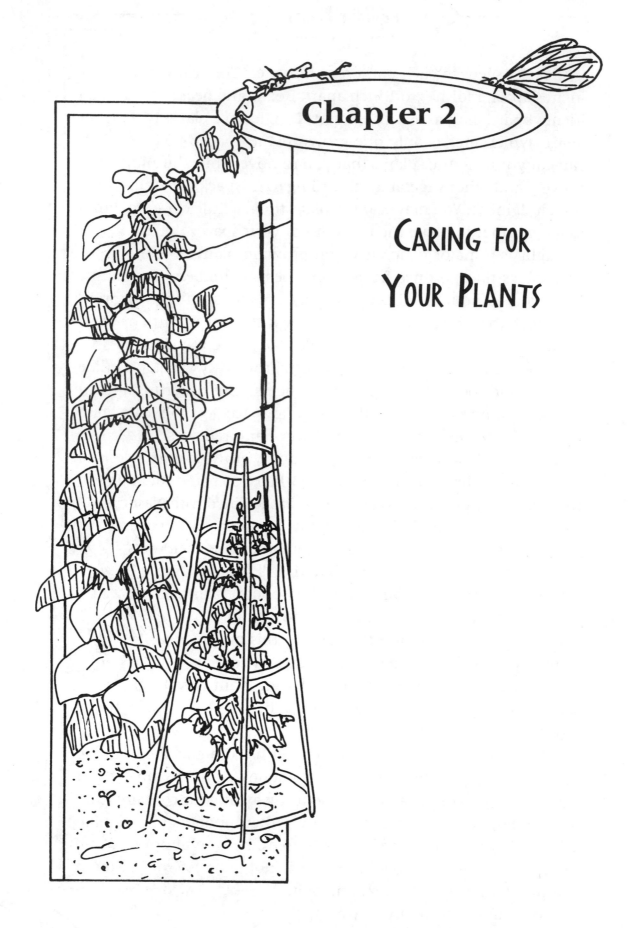

Chapter 2

CARING FOR YOUR PLANTS

WATERING THE SPROUTS

Most seeds and sprouts die in nature. They are either eaten or don't get enough water or soil. That's okay because the mother plant made thousands of them. She has thousands to spare.

You don't have so many extras. But the sprouts and young plants in your garden will be fine with just a little attention.

Seeds that are just sprouting need moisture all the time. If the soil dries out even for a short time, the sprouts will be damaged or die. You may need to water them two or three times a day until the new plants are an inch or two tall. Small seeds right on the surface of the soil are more likely to dry out than deeper ones.

I cover all my seeds with black plastic for a few days after planting. Large garbage bags split up the sides, and anchored with bricks, work fine. Or you can use a sheet of plastic from the hardware store. The plastic protects the seeds from seed-eating birds, and it also keeps the soil from drying out.

If you use plastic, be sure to peek under it every day and take it off as soon as you can see the little plants. Some types of seeds sprout sooner than others, so peek at each plot. If you don't take the plastic off the day your plants first appear, they'll quickly grow long but weak stems. This is nature's way of helping them seek light. But it doesn't make strong plants.

The plastic is most helpful with very small seeds like carrots, lettuce, snapdragons, alyssum, and impatiens. Others may be okay without it if you water frequently.

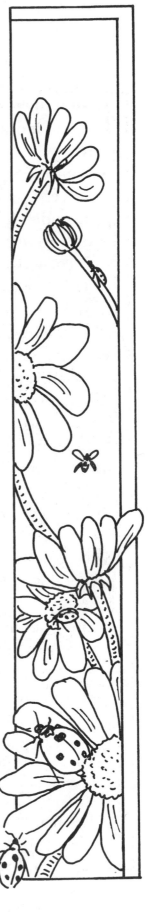

WATERING YOUNG PLANTS

How much you water depends on your climate. You'll have to figure it out by watching your plants. My friend squirts her garden briefly every day with a nozzle on the garden hose. The water only moistens the top inch of soil. Her plants look great, but they have very shallow root systems. In other words, the roots on her plants don't go down very far into the soil. Why should her plants bother to grow deep roots when all the moisture is right at the surface, and it's there every day?

Okay, so her plants have shallow roots—so what? Well, it may not be a problem if she's going to be there every day to water them (and as long as we don't have a big wind storm). Roots are anchors as well as water-gatherers.

What is a better watering strategy? Let the soil and the leaves be your guide. But don't water every day. Maybe every third day, maybe once a week. Feel the soil 2 or 3 inches down. If it feels completely dry, you probably need to water. Or if your plants are wilting at midday, then water.

I use just a garden hose with no nozzle, no sprinkler. Water sprayed on the leaves can spread plant diseases. I water until the soil is soaked several inches down. This encourages the roots to grow deep. Plants with deep roots can last longer between waterings because the soil deeper down doesn't dry out as fast as the surface soil.

An irrigation hose is one with holes poked in it. If you wind it among your plants, it waters the ground without spraying the leaves very much. Once you get it in the right place, it can save time.

And plenty of gardeners do use sprinklers. If that's easier for you, use one.

HOW DO PLANTS KNOW WHICH WAY TO GROW?

Have you ever noticed that a houseplant next to a window will turn to face the light? A plant doesn't have muscles. So how does it turn itself?

Light causes different parts of the plant to grow differently. The side of the stem away from the window grows faster than the side of the stem in the light. After awhile, the darker side of the stem is longer than the side in the light. This causes the whole plant to bend toward the light.

To see for yourself how this works, make a tube out of Play-Doh or modeling clay. Put a milk carton cap on each end to make the ends stay flat and even. Stretch one side of the tube just a little, without stretching the other side. The tube will have to bend to make room for the extra length on one side.

STAKING TOMATOES

Tomato plants usually do better if tied into an upright position. Their stems are not strong enough to hold them up.

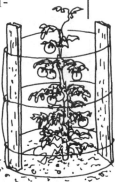

The easiest way to do this is by putting them in a circular cage of wire mesh. The holes in the mesh should be big enough to stick your hand through. The side branches of the tomato plant will grow through the mesh and hold the plant up. The cage itself may need to be supported by a wooden or metal stake driven about 1 foot into the ground and tied to the cage.

A cheaper way to support a tomato plant is by tying the main stem to a wooden stake about 5 feet long. Use strips of cloth or soft twine to tie the stem to the stake. Tie them loosely together in a figure 8, with one loop around the stem and one around the stake. This is less likely to damage the stem.

Some people cut off the side branches of a tomato plant that is tied to a stake, since side branches are not supported. But it's okay to leave them on, unless you notice that one is breaking off.

STAKING PEAS

Unless your seed packet says "bush" variety, your peas will need support too.

I support mine like this. I plant them in short rows, about 6 feet long. At the end of each row, I drive a 5-foot wooden stake into the ground. I tie heavy string between the two stakes at intervals of about 6 inches, all the way to the top. When the bean or pea plants get tall enough to reach the first string, they sometimes have to be guided to it by hand.

There are other ways to do it. One is to provide a stake for each plant to climb.

MULCH

A lot of gardeners put mulch around the base of each plant. Mulch can be grass clippings, straw, shredded leaves, pine needles, bark chips, or any similar material. It keeps the moisture from evaporating out of the soil so fast in the hot sun. It also keeps weeds from growing as fast because it blocks the light to them and also makes a barrier on the soil. A third advantage of mulch is that it keeps the roots cooler.

Some people mulch the entire garden. This is easier in a small garden than in a large one.

Mulch provides hiding places for animal life—helpers and nonhelpers. Slugs and snails, crickets, and pillbugs will hide under mulch. All of these are plant munchers. Ground beetles, worm snakes, centipedes, and salamanders, which are all predators, will also hide under mulch.

Grass clippings used as mulch will become matted together after a few rains, so you can lift up a whole area at once. This makes it easy to check for snails and slugs underneath.

WEEDING

The best way to keep weeds away is to put down a thick layer of mulch.

A weedless garden looks tidy, but a few weeds do no damage. If you decide to pull them up, you will find it easier to do it just after a rain. Wet soil is softer. If you grab the weed right next to the wet ground, you will probably be able to pull the whole plant out. If you try to pull it from dry soil, the weed will probably break off at ground level, leaving the roots in the ground. And then the roots may grow a new top. How annoying.

Be careful of pulling weeds right next to one of your garden plants. If pulling the weed tears up the soil, you may damage the roots of your garden plant.

If you want to weed a large area where there are no garden plants, it's faster to use a small shovel. Turn the soil over in chunks, break it up, and then just lift the weeds out.

A little bit of weeding every day or every other day keeps the weeds from getting out of control. Frequent weeding takes less effort on the whole because deeply rooted weeds are much harder to pull out.

FERTILIZERS

If you use compost or manure in your garden soil, you won't need chemical fertilizer. Fertilizer does supply nutrients that plants need to the soil. But it has no effect on the texture of the soil. So if your soil is too hard, has too much sand, or too much clay, fertilizer will not change that. Compost or manure will not only provide nutrients but will improve the texture of your soil too. A good texture is one that feels light and loose and almost spongy in your hand, crumbles easily, holds water well, and doesn't compact easily into a hard clod.

If you can't add compost or manure, fertilizer may be useful.

PESTICIDES

A pesticide is a substance designed to kill pests. If you are interested in the animal life of your garden, avoid chemical pesticides. Many sprays and powders will kill not only the bugs you don't want but the ones you do want as well.

There are other strategies of pest control. The most interesting is to encourage animals that eat pests. Section Four of this book describes how to do that.

Other ways to remove pests are hand-picking or spraying with a hose.

Bacillus thuringiensis, also known as Bt, is a bacterium sold under names such as Dipel or Thuricide. It will kill tomato hornworms, cabbage worms, and many other pests. But it is expensive and may also kill insects you want.

INSECT HELPERS YOU CAN BUY

You can order lacewings, ladybugs, and praying mantises to release in your garden. They are all predators that eat insect pests. Lacewings and ladybugs prey mainly on aphids. Mantises, as you'll learn in Chapter 15, will eat nearly any moving animal small enough for them to grab.

An adult green lacewing has delicate clear wings. The pale green veins on the wings are like the threads of fine lace. The lacewing, I think, is more fairylike than any other insect. Its body is pale green too and slender, about 1/2 inch long, with the wings a little longer.

Adult lacewings eat mostly nectar and will be attracted to many of the nectar flowers in this garden. The lacewing's eggs are very distinctive. She lays them one at a time, each one at the tip of a slender stalk. To make the stalk, she touches the tip of her abdomen to the underside of a leaf, leaving a dab of "glue." When she pulls her abdomen away, she draws the glue out into a stalk. It hardens quickly. On the end she places the tiny egg, which is not much bigger than the period at the end of this sentence. Why does she do that? Probably to keep the eggs away from sisters and brothers who have already hatched.

Lacewing larvae resemble tiny overturned canoes—pointed at both ends and widest in the middle. They have long needle-thin curved jaws for grabbing aphids and small caterpillars and sucking them dry. Although the larvae, even at full size, are only 1/4 inch or so, the curved jaws are powerful.

I ordered some lacewings for my garden about three years ago, and I still find them frequently. A one-minute search of the undersides of my tomato leaves turns up two to five stalked eggs. And I hardly have any aphids left. Lacewings have a good reputation for staying around long after you release them.

Ladybugs are less likely to stay around. But they can have a huge impact while they're in your garden. Both adults and larvae eat aphids. The female lays her white or yellow cigar-shaped eggs in clusters on the undersides of leaves. The larvae, which look like little alligators, have a very rough bristly surface. They can eat dozens of aphids a day.

Both kinds of larvae, lacewing and ladybug, will readily eat aphids in a dish where you can watch. A lacewing larva may pinch you, and it will hurt, even though he is tiny. I wonder what the two would do to each other. I'm sure they often cross paths in the garden.

The Garden Plants and the Helpful and Harmless Plant–Eaters

Chapter 3

NECTAR FLOWERS
FOR BUTTERFLIES

Butterflies like sugar as much as you do. In fact, sugar is the main food they need to survive. But a butterfly can only drink, not eat, because its mouth is like a soft flexible straw. So it drinks its sugar dissolved in water. You drink sugar water, with added flavorings, every time you drink soda pop. But where in nature can a butterfly find sugar water? Flowers make sugar water, called nectar, to give away to butterflies and bees and humming-birds. The nectar is a fair trade for the pollen that the creatures bring.

Can any butterfly get nectar from any flower? No. Some flowers make no nectar but rely on wind to carry pollen from flower to flower. And some flowers make much less nectar than others.

Even among the flowers that have lots of nectar, butterflies have favorites. Some flowers may taste better than others. And the flower's shape can make a difference. The petals may form a tube so long and narrow that a big butterfly can't reach the nectar, while a small butterfly can crawl right inside. In other flowers, the nectar may be easy to reach for everyone.

FISHING LINE MOUTH

I stepped outside to get the newspaper this morning and saw a butterfly perched on one of my coneflowers. It was a silver-spotted skipper. Like all butterflies at rest, she held her wings over her back so I could only see the undersides. She had her long mouthpart, her "proboscis," cast out like a fishing pole. It stuck straight out from her face for about 1/3 inch, like a pole,

then took a sharp turn down, like a fishing line. She was jerking it up and down as she searched for nectar on the coneflower, like the needle on a sewing machine. After a minute or so, she curled the proboscis back up to her face (like one of those paper party favors that uncurl when you blow in it). Then the butterfly whipped it out again, probing for nectar at breakneck speed. She didn't seem to mind how close I got as I watched. Not all butterflies are so fearless.

WHAT IS AN INSECT?

An insect is a member of the class Insecta, which includes animals having six legs, two antennae, and three main body sections—a head, thorax, and abdomen. The class Insecta is part of a larger group, the phylum Arthropoda. Arthropods are all animals having an exoskeleton and jointed legs. This includes insects. But it also includes spiders, crustaceans, millipedes, centipedes, and a few others. Spiders are arthropods because they have exoskeletons and jointed legs. But they are not insects because they have eight legs and only two main body sections.

The class Insecta includes a lot of animals in this book. It includes butterflies and moths, flies, aphids, beetles, mantises, assassin bugs, and wasps—and lots of others.

HOW IS A BUTTERFLY DIFFERENT FROM OTHER INSECTS?

Butterflies, as well as moths, belong to the insect order Lepidoptera. All these creatures have four wings, each covered with tiny scales that give the wings their color and that rub off easily. The mouth of most adults is a long coiled tube for drinking liquids. The eggs hatch into larvae, or caterpillars, that have jaws for chewing and usually three pairs of legs on the thorax. They may have up to five pairs of "prolegs" on the abdomen, which look like real legs but disappear after the larval stage.

Most caterpillars feed on plants. When fully grown, the caterpillars undergo "metamorphosis." Moths transform themselves inside a silken cocoon, or a folded leaf, or some other hiding place. Butterflies change from caterpillars to adults inside a little package of skin called a "chrysalis."

Adult moths are usually active by night and adult butterflies by day. Butterflies tend to be more colorful and more appreciated, but the moths are a larger and more diverse group.

PLANTING THE FLOWERS

You will find six types of flowers on the "Garden Map" (see page iv) for butterflies. Buy the alyssum and ageratum as young plants if you can find them. The zinnias and marigolds grow easily from seed but may also be available as young plants. The coneflowers and hollyhocks you will probably have to start from seed, as young plants may be hard to find. These last two are both tall. Hollyhocks will need to be tied to wooden stakes, a wall, or to your house as they grow. The ageratum, alyssum, zinnias, and marigolds are shorter.

Possible substitutions, all good butterfly flowers, are aster, black-eyed Susan, heliotrope, lantana, lobelia, morning glory, nasturtium, nicotiana, phlox, sweet William, and verbena.

Which Color to Choose?

Some lepidopterists (butterfly scientists) will tell you that butterflies prefer flowers of yellow and especially purple color. Others disagree. You can give butterflies a choice of colors and decide for yourself.

To test the purple theory, you can plant a bed of purple coneflowers next to a bed of white coneflowers, as shown in the "Garden Map." Or you could use alyssum instead, which also comes in both purple and white.

As for the colors of your other butterfly flowers, I would choose bright yellow, golds, and purples. But that is up to you.

THE CLOUDY DAY TEST

Many people believe that butterflies fly around more on sunny days than on cloudy days. Could this be true, or is it just that we think of butterflies as happy sunny creatures?

Write down how many butterflies you see on sunny warm days and how many on cloudy warm days when you can't see the sun, but it isn't raining. Can you think of any reason why butterflies might prefer sunny days? (Remember that all insects are cold-blooded. This means that their temperature changes with the air around them.)

22

SUGARY SNACKS

We know that butterflies like nectar, but will they take sugar in any other form? Some may eat rotting fruit. Put a slice of watermelon, cantaloupe, or peach near your flower bed. You can also offer them "mothing sugar," a mixture that moths like and probably butterflies too. Here's one recipe:

2 cups sugar
1/4 cup stale beer
1 mashed overripe banana
1 tablespoon molasses or syrup
a slosh of fruit juice

You can vary the amounts as needed to make the mixture a paste, not a liquid. Put some of the mixture on a sponge and place it in the yard near your flowers, and perhaps on a table, away from dogs.

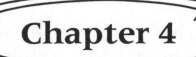

Chapter 4

Nectar Flowers for Hummingbirds

Like their fluttery friends the butterflies, hummingbirds drink sugary nectar from flowers. They have very long slender bills that can reach into the longest tubular flowers, even those too deep and narrow for butterflies and bees. Hummingbirds spread pollen from flower to flower as they move about, just as butterflies, bees, and hover flies do.

HOW ARE HUMMINGBIRDS DIFFERENT FROM OTHER BIRDS?

Hummers (hummingbirds) are the smallest of all birds in North America. Their long thin bills are different from other birds' bills, and their flight pattern is too. They can move their wings in a figure 8 that enables them to hover and to even fly backwards. Hummingbirds' wings beat so fast that they make a humming sound and look blurred.

AREN'T HUMMERS MORE LIKE INSECTS THAN BIRDS?

If hummingbirds are so small and eat nectar, why don't we just classify them as insects? Some moths are as big as hummingbirds, and they eat nectar too. Hummingbirds are even sometimes eaten by spiders or by praying mantises. Why do we classify something so small with the birds?

A couple of big reasons. One is that hummingbirds have feathers. All birds have feathers, and no other animals do. So if an animal has feathers, it's a bird—period. But aside from that, hummingbirds have an internal skeleton of bones. So they are vertebrates, as are all birds, mammals, reptiles, amphibians, and fish. Insects have an external skeleton, or exoskeleton—no bones.

PLANTING THE FLOWERS

Here is a list of six flowers that you can plant to attract hummingbirds to your garden: petunias, snapdragons, impatiens, trumpet vine, clematis, and trumpet honeysuckle. Young petunia plants are available at nearly any store selling garden plants. Easy to grow, the plants stay low to the ground. Impatiens and snapdragons can be hard to get started from seed, so buy young plants if you can. Both are usually less than knee high when grown.

The next three plants are all vines. You should buy them as plants, not seeds, because they take a long time to grow. Each plant comes in a 1-gallon container. You may find them in smaller containers, but bigger plants will bloom sooner. All three vines are more expensive than the other plants in this book.

Trumpet vine, or trumpet creeper, is a hummingbird favorite, with large trumpet-shaped orange flowers. The vine needs something like a wall or fence to climb. A stump or tree may do. Its clingy tendrils, sort of like roots above ground, can damage paint. It can also get very heavy. You may have to call two or three nurseries to find trumpet vine. Plant it as early as the nursery recommends. If you don't plant it early, it will probably not bloom the first year.

Clematis has huge showy flowers and also likes to climb. But it climbs by intertwining rather than clinging, so it doesn't damage paint. It will grow up a mailbox post, a fence, or a trellis, which is a delicate sort of fence just for plants to climb, made of criss-crossed wooden slats. Clematis is more likely than trumpet vine to bloom the first year you plant it. But get at least the 1-gallon size, and look for one that is already blooming in the pot. Ask at the nursery for advice in selecting one—there are many different species of clematis. Ask also for particular planting instructions.

Trumpet honeysuckle will climb the same sorts of structures clematis climbs. It is a twining vine, not a clinging one. It's not as heavy as trumpet vine and is more likely to bloom the first year you plant it. The flowers are red and tubular, smaller than the flowers of trumpet vine.

Other hummingbird favorites, for substitutions, are bee balm, columbine, coral-bell, daylily, delphin-ium, fuchsia, lantana, lupine, nasturtium, nicotiana, pent-stemon, phlox, and red salvia.

27

THE SUGAR TEST

Sugar dissolved in water is not visible. You can make it visible by evaporating the water. Put a few drops of sugar water on a dark plate. Check it after a few days. Do you see the sugar crystals? Do the same with a clear soft drink. Now do it again with a drop of nectar gathered from several honeysuckle flowers. What do you see?

PURPLE AND YELLOW FOR HUMMERS TOO?

If butterflies like purple and yellow, does that mean hummingbirds do too? Maybe not. Many birders claim that hummingbirds like red and orange best! You can test them for yourself and see, in the same way that Chapter 3 suggested testing butterflies. Plant red and white beds of the same flower side by side. (See the "Garden Map" on page iv.) You could use impatiens or petunias; both of these come in both red and white. Record the number of hummers you see in each plot.

Fake Flowers

Another way to test the color idea is to lure hummingbirds with fake flowers. Begin by planting two identical beds of hummingbird flowers, in separate parts of the garden. The two beds are the same flower type and the same color (any color except red or orange). Then make two big fake flowers for the two beds—one red and one white or blue. You can cut two flower shapes from plastic lids of ice cream containers. Cover your plastic flowers with colored waterproof tape. Place the red plastic flower in an easily seen spot in one bed, the white or blue flower in the other bed. In which flower bed do you first see a hummingbird? You can make feeders with these plastic flowers if you know someone who can get you a glass tube from a doctor's office or science shop. Cut a hole in the plastic flower to fit around the top of the tube, and fill the tube with sugar water (1/4 cup sugar, 1 quart water).

Be a Flower

If you have a lot of hummingbirds, wear a red shirt and sit outside quietly at a time you think they might visit. Hummers sometimes will come quite close to an object that catches their attention, even close enough to investigate red lipstick!

Chapter 5

Nectar and Pollen for Hover Flies

Hover flies are our most important pollinators, second only to bees. Then how come you've never heard of them? You've probably seen lots of them but thought they were bees or wasps. Most kinds of hover flies have patterns that imitate these guys—stripes of yellow and black, or white and brown. Insect-eating birds connect these patterns with painful stings and leave the hover flies alone. Hover flies have no sting, though, and are completely harmless.

So how can you tell a hover fly from a wasp or bee? Like all flies, hover flies have only two wings. These two wings stick out from the insect's sides a bit at rest. All wasps and bees are different. They have four wings, which close over the back and don't stick out much.

Hover flies are the helicopters of the insect world. They are experts at flying in one place, or hovering. Bees and wasps can hover too, but they will waver, or bob up and down a little. A hover fly will seem to freeze in midair. It may then move a few inches and freeze again. The fly manages to stay completely still, in spite of air currents, by watching one object. It makes the flight adjustments necessary to keep the object in the same relative position. Tricky.

FLOWERS FOR FLOWER FLIES

Hover flies are sometimes called flower flies. They fly from flower to flower, eating nectar and sometimes pollen. Three nectar-rich flowers you can plant for hover flies are cosmos, marigolds, and coreopsis.

Cosmos and marigolds grow easily from packets of seeds. Almost every nursery carries young marigold plants, though. They're not expensive, and they're a good choice if you want to get a head start by setting out young plants instead of seeds. Cosmos and marigolds come in lots of colors. Consider choosing the colors that have been suggested for butterfly and hover fly color preference tests (see Chapter 3 and page 33). These colors are blues, purples, yellows, and golds.

Coreopsis is a plant that will survive all winter and live for years. Such plants are called perennials. They cost more as plants than the ones that live only one summer, like cosmos and marigolds. For that reason, you'll probably want to start coreopsis from seeds.

See the "Garden Map" on page iv for where to start these plants.

Just How Sweet?

Most nectar eaters are attracted to sugar and water, which is very similar to nectar. When I was on a picnic recently, a hover fly landed on my Tootsie Roll wrapper. There was a bit of brown goo on the wrapper. The fly unfurled his sucking mouthpart, which looked somewhat like a short elephant's trunk, and had a go at the goo. But it was too thick for him. I put a drop of water on it, stirred it around with a stem, and he slurped it right up like a vacuum cleaner hose. He didn't seem to mind my fooling around with his lunch.

Will any sort of sugar mixture do? How particular are they? You can do an experiment and find out. You can offer mixtures of water with different amounts of sugar. Get four saucers of the same color, size, and shape. Make the four suggested mixtures of water and sugar, stirring each until all the sugar is dissolved. Then put into each saucer a couple of tablespoons of one of the mixtures.

Mixture #1: 1/8 teaspoon of granulated sugar and 1 cup of water
Mixture #2: 1/2 teaspoon of granulated sugar and 1 cup of water

Mixture #3: 1 teaspoon of granulated sugar and 1 cup of water
Mixture #4: 3 teaspoons of granulated sugar and 1 cup of water

Put the saucers side by side on a table outdoors on a warm sunny day. Record how many hover flies visit each saucer. Bees and butterflies, and even hummingbirds, may visit your saucers as well. You may want to record their numbers as well.

Another option is to put different sorts of sweet liquids, instead of sugar mixtures, into your saucers. You could try honey, a soft drink, pancake syrup, molasses, Kool-Aid, or just plain water. Try adding something bitter or sour, like quinine or lemon juice, to one of your sweet liquids. Does it make a difference?

If you don't get any visitors at first, you can put a sheet of brightly colored paper under the dishes. What color? Read on and see.

Colors

Do hover flies, like butterflies and hummingbirds, have color preferences? You can find out with different colors of paper. One way to go about it is to offer color choices on a single notebook-sized sheet of paper. Trim one end of the paper to make it a square. Now with a pencil and a ruler divide your square into nine smaller squares of equal size. Pick four of those squares at random (not ones that are side by side). Color two of them medium blue and two of them yellow. These are colors that have been reported to attract hover flies. The other squares may be white or other colors. Glue or tape your sheet on a piece of cardboard to keep it from blowing away outside.

Another way to do this is to make about ten squares of differently colored construction paper—a couple bright blue and a couple yellow. Each should be at least the size of an average flower. A little bigger is better. They don't need to be connected.

Now place your squares near a flower bed and watch from a distance. Record how many hover flies *land* on each color. (Hovering over it doesn't count!) Do they have a preference? Do bees and butterflies visit your colors as well?

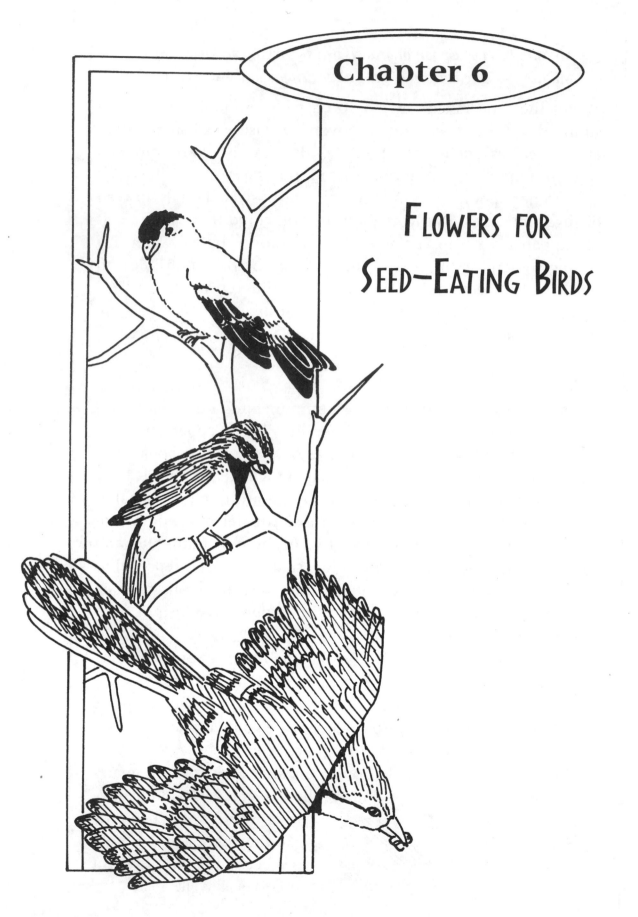

Chapter 6

FLOWERS FOR SEED-EATING BIRDS

PLANT REPRODUCTION

A plant has sex organs, just as humans and animals do. But where? Under the branches? No, the female organs and male organs are inside the flowers. A female organ, called a "pistil," has tiny eggs inside it. A flower's male organs produce a yellow powder called "pollen." If the eggs in the pistil are fertilized by pollen, then the eggs will become seeds. And a seed, as you know, can grow into a new plant. It's similar to the way a fertilized egg inside a woman's body will grow into a baby— a new human.

But even though a single plant may have both male and female parts, even in the same flower, a plant can't fertilize its own eggs. So the plant has a problem—how can it reach the pollen from another plant, which may be far away? Plants can't move, of course, having no muscles. The solution is that animals bring the pollen to them! The flowers make sugar water, called nectar, that bees, butterflies, hover flies, and hummingbirds love. And as these critters travel from one flower to another, drinking the nectar, they accidentally brush up against the pollen and carry it with them. (Just as you sometimes carry sand indoors stuck on your clothes or shoes.) The pollen on the little creature's body sticks to the female parts on the next flower. So that's how plants get the pollen they need to make seeds.

What happens once the pollen is on the female organ, the pistil? Inside each pollen grain are two sperm cells. They have to get from the outside of the pistil to the inside, where the eggs are. To do this, they have to travel down the long middle part of the pistil, called the "style." That's a long way for a couple of tiny sperm cells! How can they do it? To help them, the pollen grain grows a long skinny tube that reaches all the way down the style to the ovary. The two sperm cells swim down the tube and finally reach the eggs.

When pollen gets to the eggs inside a flower, each egg forms a seed. A seed is a baby plant, like a kitten or a baby human still inside its mother. Until the seeds ripen, they need to stay attached to the parent plant. So tell your mom not to tidy up the garden by plucking all the flowers that look dead! The seeds inside those flowers are alive! The petals may look dead, and they are, because their job is done. Their job has been to serve as colorful flags to attract the pollen bringers—the bees, butterflies, hover flies, and hummingbirds. Once the pollen has arrived and the seeds have started to form, the color is no longer needed. So the petals wither and fall off.

When animals mate, do the male's sperm face a similar problem of how to get inside the female, where the eggs are? Evolution has solved this problem differently for different types of animals. Mammals have a different solution than birds have, for example. Animals or plants that live in water, like fish or sea urchins or algae, can just dump their sperm and eggs in the water and let fertilization happen there. But we animals and plants that live on land must protect our eggs from drying out, so fertilization must happen internally.

Are animals' and plants' solutions to survival problems, like how to get sperm and egg together, so very different? Not as different as you might think. If you study biology, you'll learn that our solutions and plants' solutions are often surprisingly similar.

SEEDS FOR THE BIRDS

What happens to all those seeds? Some plants make hundreds. Songbirds and mice eat a lot of them. The sunflowers, cosmos, and zinnias in this garden have been included because their seeds are especially tasty to songbirds. All are easy to grow from seeds. Zinnias are also easy to find as young plants and don't cost much. (Other flowers you could substitute are ageratum, aster, bachelor's button, California poppy, cleome, columbine, coreopsis, globe thistle, goldenrod, and scabiosa.) The sunflowers, which are very tall, should be placed along the north end of the garden to avoid shading other plants. The cosmos and zinnias should be placed away from shrubs or other possible hiding places for cats. Cats kill a tremendous number of songbirds.

The sunflower will attract finches, sparrows, jays, cardinals (in the east) and others. Goldfinches and sparrows will enjoy the zinnias. The cosmos is a particular favorite of goldfinches, who will hang onto the flowers with their feet while removing the seeds.

HOUSE CATS AND BIRDS

You probably know that house cats kill squirrels, chipmunks, and songbirds. If you have a cat, you may have caught it with prey before.

One of my friends has a cat. My friend knows that her cat kills birds. But because the cat is well-fed at home, she says he doesn't kill very many birds. He's not hungry, so he doesn't need to kill many.

It would be nice if that were true. But it's not true. Cats don't kill because they're hungry. They kill because the sight of prey brings out the instinct to stalk and capture. They hunt just as much when they are well-fed at home as when they are hungry. In fact, they hunt more successfully when they *are* well-fed at home. Why? Because a strong healthy predator is a more effective predator.

Scientists in the state of Wisconsin and in England have been studying cats' outdoor activities. The scientists put collars with radio transmitters on a large number of cats, which allowed them to track the cats' movements. They found that each house cat kills between 100 and 1,000 small animals per year! In Wisconsin, cats are killing hundreds of millions of birds and small mammals each year. The problem exists in every state, not just Wisconsin. In some areas, house cats have completely wiped out populations of particular songbirds.

In planning your garden, be sure to get rid of all cat hideouts near your seed flowers and bird feeders. Or else your feathered guests could be a killer kitty's next victim.

THE BIRD TASTE TEST

After you've noticed dead petals, check some of the flower heads—the part of the flower that remains after the petals. The flower heads contain the seeds. When the seeds ripen, the flower head will sometimes crumble easily in your hand, separating into dozens of small seeds. Ripe sunflower seeds are mostly black. You can store them in an envelope for months, until planting time next spring. Or you can hold on to them for the "bird taste test" to find out which seed type birds like best. Which do you think they will?

For this test, collect mature seeds from your zinnias, cosmos, and sunflowers. Place equal amounts of seeds in three identical jar lids (one seed type per lid). Put the lids on a small table in your backyard or garden, away from hiding places for cats. Watch the lids, and check them every few hours, or every day. Keep records of any birds you see eating. Which seed type is eaten first? Do all types of birds have the same favorites?

39

THE WIND TEST

Put a single seed of each type in front of you on your kitchen table, all in a row, all the same distance from you. Now get a yardstick or a long ruler and lay it on the table so that one end is in line with the seeds. Predict how far you think you can blow each seed. Use a drinking straw to blow each seed as far as you can with one breath. Which goes farthest? Measure the distance with the yardstick. Which of the seeds do you think are designed to be carried to new growing places by the wind? Which seeds are the most dried out? How does losing water help them travel faster?

THE GARDEN PLANTS AND THE HARMFUL PLANT-EATERS

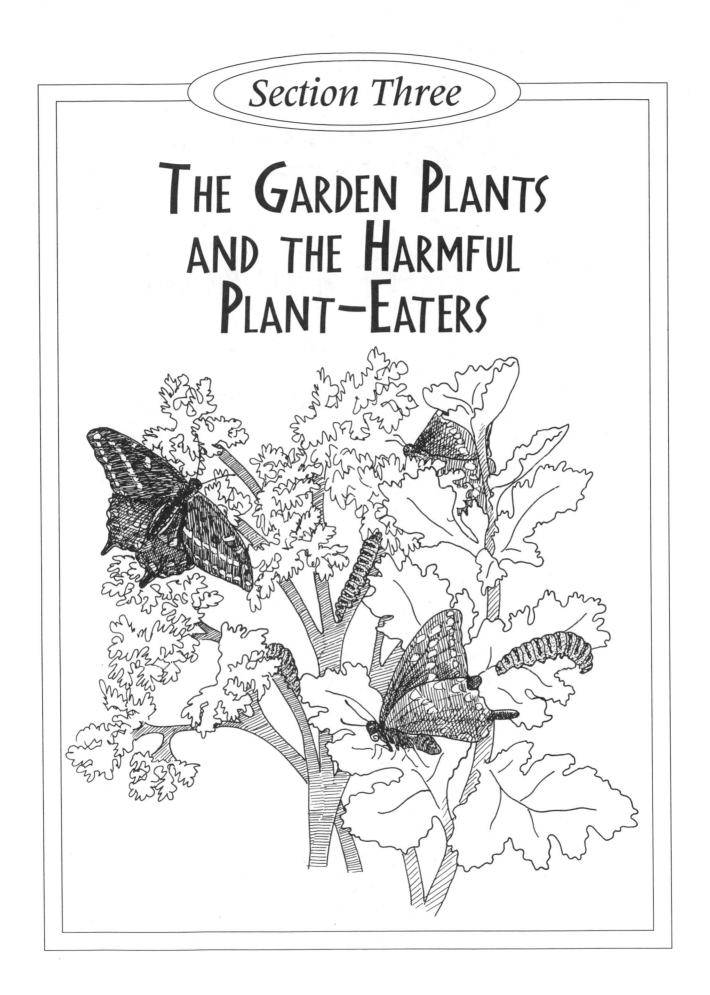

Chapter 7

PUMPKINS, CUCUMBERS, AND SUGAR PEAS ATTACKED BY APHIDS

Aphids are tiny, pear-shaped insects likely to live on your pumpkins, cucumbers, and sugar peas as well as your lettuce and tomatoes. (See also Chapter 9.) They especially like young and tender plant parts. Look on the undersides of new leaves. Most aphids are green and no bigger than the head of a pin. They can also be red, pink, yellow, gray, or other colors.

PLANTING YOUR APHID FOOD

Pumpkins, cucumbers, and sugar peas are all easy to grow from seeds. The seeds are big and not as delicate as many smaller ones. But you can also buy them as young plants already started. They're not expensive. Sugar pea plants will need something to cling to as they grow, to hold them off the ground. (See Chapter 2 for instructions.) Cucumbers and pumpkins grow on the ground and don't need support.

WHERE ARE THE GUYS?

Some aphid populations are all girls! No fathers and no brothers. Just unmated mothers giving birth to only girls. A population of only girls grows twice as fast. Every adult gives birth! Because of this strategy, aphids are one of the fastest reproducing insects in the world. As you will see with the "Aphid Babies Game," a single mother aphid can fill an entire plant with her descendants in just a few weeks. In fact, aphids can be major pests—destroying entire crops.

JABBING THE PLANTS

What are they doing under the leaves? Stabbing the plants with their long, strawlike mouthparts and sucking out the plant's juices. Ouch!

You can temporarily get rid of aphids by spraying them with a mixture of water and a little bit of liquid soap, which won't hurt the plant. Try it.

Sometimes just hosing the plants with plain water will knock off all the aphids, as will a heavy rainstorm. But they'll be back in a day or two.

OTHER INSECT SUCKERS

Aphids belong to an order of insects called "Homoptera," which includes also cicadas, leafhoppers, treehoppers, planthoppers, mealybugs, scale bugs and others. All are plant-eaters with sucking, beaklike mouthparts. Homoptera means "similar wing," a name given to this group because the wings are all clear. This trait separates the Homoptera from their close relatives, the Hemiptera, whose wings are part leathery and part clear. The Hemiptera are all suckers too, but they don't all suck plants. So what do they suck? You'll meet one of the most murderous hemipterans, the assassin bug, in Chapter 19. This is one awesome insect.

THE APHID BABIES GAME

Draw and color a big leaf on each of three sheets of paper. To play you can use pennies or dried beans on your leaves to represent aphids. Each aphid (penny) is going to give birth to ten more aphids (pennies). If you start with one aphid, how many generations do you think it will take to fill up your leaves? Make a prediction before you begin.

Here's how you start: Put one penny, your first mother aphid, on one of your leaves. She is the first generation. This mother aphid gives birth to ten babies (ten pennies). These ten babies are the second generation. Put them on the mother's leaf. Each one of these pennies grows up in one week and gives birth to ten babies of her own, a third generation. Put the third generation of pennies on the leaf. How many pennies do you have on your leaf now? (One penny for the first mother aphid, generation one. Ten pennies for her daughters, generation two. And 10 x 10 pennies for her granddaughters, generation three.)

Now each aphid in generation three gives birth to ten daughters, generation four. Put down a penny for each aphid in generation four. Are you running out of pennies yet? Are your leaves filled up? How do your results compare to your prediction?

How many aphids would be in generation five? Generation six? How many weeks are there in your growing season?

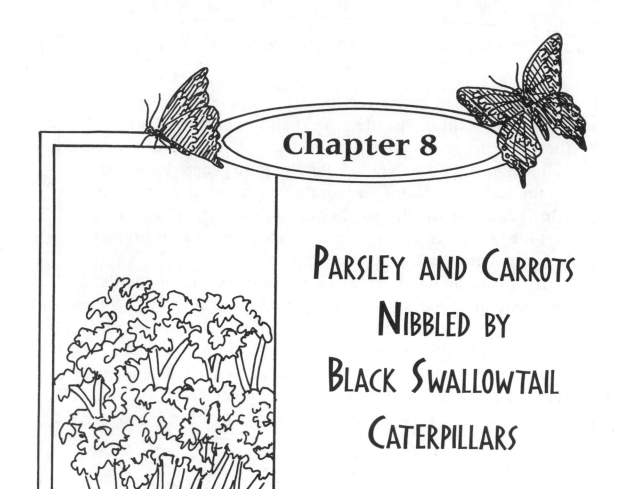

Chapter 8

Parsley and Carrots Nibbled by Black Swallowtail Caterpillars

A baby butterfly is a caterpillar. You learned in Chapter 3 that adult butterflies need sugar to eat, which they get from the nectar of flowers. Sugar is a high-energy food, good for flying around. But caterpillars have a lot of growing to do. They need salad, not sugar. So they eat leafy foods. Each type of caterpillar needs a specific type of leaf. The caterpillar of the black swallowtail butterfly eats the leaves of carrots and parsley (a carrot relative).

STARTING YOUR CARROTS AND PARSLEY

Carrots and parsley grow from very tiny seeds. When your soil is ready, sprinkle the tiny seeds on top. Water them very gently but thoroughly. Because the seeds are so small, the first sprouts from the seeds are very small too. They can dry out and die very easily. So it is especially important with carrot seeds to cover them with a sheet of black plastic for the first few days, as they sprout. Garbage bags that have been split up the seams will do, or you can get a sheet of plastic from the hardware store. Anchor the corners of the plastic with bricks or rocks. Check under the plastic every day. The plants will be very tiny at first, the size of one letter on this page. As soon as you see any of them, remove the plastic right away. Then keep the soil damp.

Carrots must be grown from seed. But you can buy parsley that is already growing. Carrots can be planted one month before most flowers and warm-weather vegetables such as tomatoes, which must wait until the danger of frost has passed.

GROWING CATERPILLARS

The more carrots and parsley you have, the more likely you are to get black swallowtail caterpillars. Having nectar flowers from Chapter 3 to attract and feed the adults will also increase your chances of getting caterpillars. The mother butterfly lays her eggs on plants in the carrot family. The caterpillar is mostly green, with narrow black crossbands. The black bands have yellow marks on them. As it grows, the caterpillar will shed its skin several times. When grown, it will usually leave the carrot or parsley in search of a place to turn itself into a butterfly. This metamorphosis occurs inside a little package of skin called a "chrysalis" and takes about two weeks.

If you do not find any caterpillars in your garden, you may find some on Queen Anne's lace (a wildflower in the carrot family—smell its roots). You can move them gently to your carrots or parsley.

Find a Perch for the Metamorphosis

When your caterpillars are grown, you can offer them some choices about where to settle themselves for the big change. They like a firm surface to which they can attach the chrysalis, with a bit of glue and silk from their bodies. You can offer them branches, posts, bricks, or plant stalks stuck firmly in the ground near carrots or parsley. When your caterpillars are large, check each branch or stalk every day for a chrysalis. An hour or so before the butterfly emerges, the chrysalis may become darker or clear, so that you can see parts of the butterfly. It emerges headfirst, with crumpled wings. During the first hour, the wings straighten and harden. After this time, the butterfly may be willing to stand briefly on your finger. Move slowly, and do not touch its wings, which are covered with delicate colored scales. Offer the butterfly a little sugar water (a LITTLE sugar) soaked in paper. If it is not interested, place its hind "feet" on the sweet area. (This is how they taste.) A caged butterfly will damage its wings fluttering at the sides. Evening, when insect-eating birds are resting, is the safest time for setting it free.

Chapter 9

Lettuce and Cherry Tomatoes Munched by Slugs and Snails

If you've ever had a bed of baby lettuce disappear overnight, slugs were probably to blame. Slugs like tender young plants of almost any type, but lettuce is probably a favorite. Tender fruits are another favorite, like tomatoes and strawberries. (Did you know that tomatoes are actually fruits?) Snails will scrape the skin off a tomato, but slugs will eat holes in them.

How Is a Slug Like an Octopus?

Snails and slugs are mollusks, not insects. The phylum Mollusca includes clams, oysters, and scallops, as well as octopuses and squids. What do all these animals have in common? Well, for one thing, none of them have an internal skeleton, like we do. Some of them do have shells on the outside of their bodies.

All mollusks have bodies with these three basic parts: head, muscular foot, and internal organs. The muscular foot of a slug or snail is the part of it that comes in contact with the ground. It's the part that moves the creature along from one place to the next and leaves a slime trail. If you put a slug on a sheet of glass, you can see the rhythmic, wave-like contractions of the foot from underneath. In a clam or oyster, the muscular foot is the part that sticks out of the two-sided shell and pokes down into the sand or mud to anchor the animal. The muscular foot of a squid or octopus has been changed through evolutionary time into tentacles for grabbing prey or exploring the sea bottom. Isn't it neat how the same building blocks can be changed into such different final products?

A slug looks like it has a short cape thrown over its shoulders. That part of it is called the "mantle." The mantle covers the slug's lungs. The slug can pull its head under the mantle for protection.

Look at the side of a slug's body. You'll see a hole about the size of a tomato seed. The slug breathes through that hole. On the big leopard slugs in my yard, the hole is on the right side.

A slug has two sets of tentacles on its head. The front pair is shorter. You'll notice that the slug taps these on the ground as it moves along. The longer pair of tentacles have eyes on top. If you look closely, you'll see a tiny black dot at the tip of each longer tentacle. That's the eye itself.

STARTING YOUR PLANTS

If you grow your lettuce from the seed, you'll get a lot more lettuce than if you buy young plants. Sow the seeds on top of the soil and water them gently. Lettuce seeds are small and will sprout better if you protect them with a sheet of black plastic for two to five days. Look under it every day. Remove it as soon as you see that a few seeds are growing.

Most gardeners buy cherry tomatoes as young plants rather than seeds. They will probably need to be tied to wooden stakes or a wire cage to hold them upright (see Chapter 2).

TEST THESE SLUG BARRIERS

How do you keep slugs off your new lettuce? You can test these remedies that other gardeners sometimes use. Do they work? Which is best? Beside your lettuce plot, plant these four tiny separate test plots of lettuce, each about 6 inches across.

Around test plot #1 sprinkle powdered ginger, available at any grocery store. (Ginger may be too expensive—ask your parents.) Sprinkle fresh sawdust around test plot #2. Surround test plot #3 with a barrier of vertical window screening, about 4 inches tall, sunk an inch or two in the ground. The top edge of your little screen fence should be rough. Put no protection around test plot #4. Let the slugs go at it. This is so you'll have something to compare your other test plots to. If the slugs don't eat the unprotected lettuce, then we can't say much about how useful the ginger and sawdust and screen fence are.

There are other substances you can use to steer slugs and snails away from your plants. You can substitute these for any of the barriers in the test plots. One is wood ashes. Some gardeners mix ashes with sawdust; some use ashes alone. Another is lime, which is a white powder that some gardeners mix with their garden soil in case the soil is too acidic. Sprinkle the ashes or lime in a circle around the test plot, just as you would the ginger or sawdust. Or you can also use for one of your test plots a mixture of equal amounts of vinegar and water (for example, 1 cup water and 1 cup vinegar). Spray this mixture right on the lettuce plants in one test plot. It won't hurt the plants when sprayed on, but it will if you pour it on their roots, so be careful.

One last option is a barrier of copper sheeting or paper that is covered with copper on one side. This should stand upright and encircle the test plot, just as the vertical window screening would. It may need to be stapled to a wooden stake to hold it up.

Any of these slug barriers will need to be replaced after a heavy rain, except for the window screening or copper sheeting.

DIATOMACEOUS EARTH

A diatom is a microscopic animal that lives in the ocean. Diatoms make tiny prickly skeletons out of a hard substance called "silica." When the animal dies, the skeleton remains behind. Diatomaceous earth is made of millions of these skeletons. It looks like fine dust, but each particle is very sharp. When soft-bodied animals, like slugs and caterpillars, crawl over it, it pricks and damages their skin and kills them. Diatomaceous earth is a popular remedy for garden varmints because it isn't poisonous to humans. You can buy it at garden stores. Usually it is sprinkled over the leaves of garden plants.

You could use it as a slug barrier in one of your test plots. But it is harmful to breathe—gardeners wear dust masks when using it.

So I don't recommend it for children's use, unless closely super-vised by an adult.

SLUG AND SNAIL HIDING PLACES

You may notice that you're far more likely to step on a slug at night than during the day. They wander about looking for food only at night. Where do slugs and snails go during the day? On the "Garden Map" on page iv, you'll notice boards set about the gar-den on the ground. Slugs and snails are likely to hide under these boards during the day. Do the same individuals come to the same hiding places every day? One way scientists keep track of indi-viduals is by marking them. You can easily mark snails without hurting them. Put a dab of Wite-Out or fingernail polish or model airplane paint on some of the snails you discover. Make the mark on each snail different by marking a different area of the shell or by making two or three spots on some individuals or by making marks of different shapes. Don't make big marks though. Some of the paint might soak through the shell and injure the animal. Or it might make the snail more visible to predators. Keep a record of each individual's mark and of its hiding place. Check each day after you mark the snails and see if individuals return to the same spots for their daily snooze.

SLUG AND SNAIL REMOVAL

If you want to remove slugs and snails from your garden, you can catch them in their hiding places during the day and release them elsewhere. Keep one or two for a memory test. (See below.)

SLUG MEMORY TEST

Scientists say that slugs use slime trails to find their way back to the "best" eating places. To see if this is true, place an old damp board in a cardboard box. Put a few baby lettuce leaves or a fresh strawberry or tomato slice on one end of the board. Put the slug in the middle. In a dimly lit room, watch the slug until it has found the lettuce or the strawberry. Then put it back in the middle of the board and put the lettuce, strawberry, or tomato slice at the other end of the board. Does the slug return first to the end where the food was originally? Does it travel along the old slime trail? Or does the slug go right to the food in the new location?

SLUGS AND MILK

You may have heard of setting out dishes of beer to drown slugs. They do like beer, although it gets them drunk and often kills them. But did you know that many types of slugs like milk just as well? Milk won't hurt them. If you set out a dish of milk near your garden every night, you may get regular visitors. Try it. Then try not setting the dish out one evening, and see if your regular visitors come looking for it. They may circle the area. If you listen very carefully, you may hear them calling irritably, "Hey! Where's the milk?"

HERMAPHRODITES

Did you know that each snail and slug is both a girl and a boy? How can that be? Each one has both female and male sex organs, or reproductive parts. Whoa! How confusing! Why would nature do such a thing? Because slugs and snails are very slow, and they're solitary. They hang out alone. When it's time to mate, it can take a very long time to find another individual of the same species. What if Pat the Slug was a boy, slugging along looking for someone to make babies with? Ah, finally! Here comes another slug! Oh shoot. The new slug is another boy. He can't produce offspring with Pat. Two days later Pat comes upon one more slug. But it's another boy again. Pat is outta luck.

Now imagine Pat the hermaphrodite, both boy and girl in one. This Pat is also looking for a mate. Pat is cruising along through your garden and sees another slug, Chris. No problem. Chris is just right. Any slug Pat met would be just right. Pat says to Chris, "You fertilize my eggs, and I'll fertilize yours." Chris agrees. And the deal is done. No more searching.

Earthworms are hermaphrodites too and for the very same reason. They're slow, they're solitary, and they don't meet up with other worms very often. Having two sexes in one doubles the chances of being able to reproduce with the next worm they meet, when the time comes.

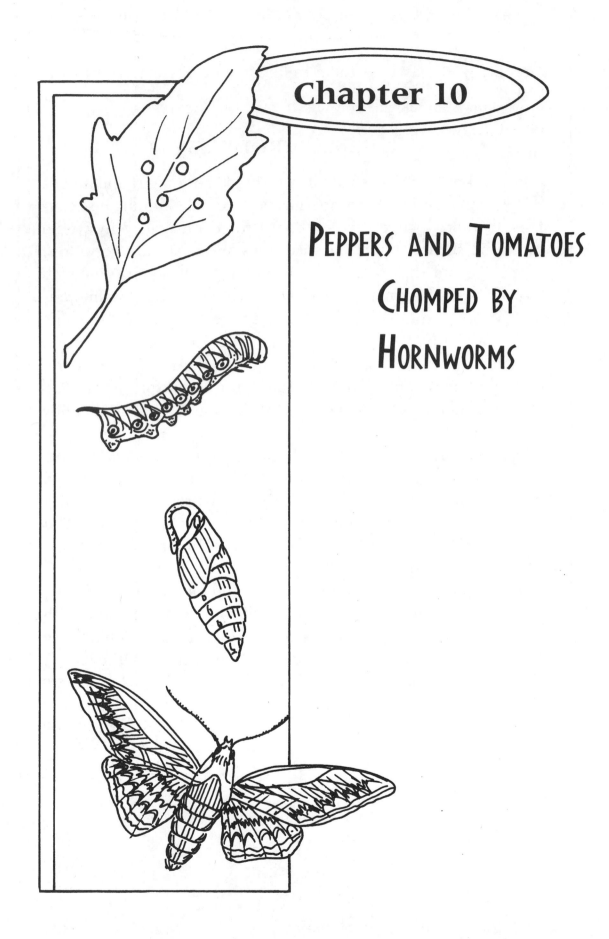

Chapter 10

Peppers and Tomatoes Chomped by Hornworms

Tomato hornworms are huge green caterpillars that grow to be 4 inches long. That's bigger than a grown-man's largest finger—pretty big for a caterpillar! They have seven or eight diagonal white stripes down the sides, with a "false eye" spot beside each stripe. (Spots that look like eyes can sometimes frighten predators away.)

One type of hornworm has a big red horn on his rear end, another type has a big black horn. Some people are afraid of the horn. But hornworms can't bite or sting. They'll try to scare you though by wagging their sharp-looking horns at you.

A tomato hornworm is the larva or caterpillar of a sphinx moth. That's a big brown moth with a wingspan of almost 5 inches. They are sometimes called hawk moths because of their powerful swooping flight.

In late spring, the moth lays single (not clumped) green eggs on the underside of tomato leaves. When the caterpillars first hatch, they are too small to notice. As they grow and chew up your tomatoes, you'll begin to see their dark green droppings on the tomato leaves and on the ground. You can pick the caterpillars off by hand to keep them from destroying your tomatoes. Keep some for the experiments that follow. You may want to have one tomato plant set apart from the others (see the "Garden Map" on page iv), which you can donate completely to the caterpillars. Hopefully they will attract the hornworm parasites described in Chapter 20.

STARTING THE PLANTS

You'll probably want to buy your green peppers and tomatoes as bedding plants. They don't cost much. You save a lot of time if you start with plants rather than seeds. Follow the planting directions that come with the plants.

The tomatoes will need to be supported somehow when they get 1 to 2 feet tall. See Chapter 2 for instructions on staking them or using a circular cage to hold them up.

WHICH DINNER?

Plant two tomato plants, one green pepper plant, and one green bean plant in the four corners of a container that is big enough for all four plants. When the plants are about a foot tall, put two to four hornworms in the center of the container with the plants. Which plants do the hornworms begin to eat first? Do all of them make the same choice? If you move one to a different plant, does it stay where you put it?

DOES IT TICKLE THE SECOND TIME?

If you are busy working in a place where soft music is playing, you may not notice the music after awhile. Or if you wear yellow-tinted sunglasses for a couple of hours, you may soon forget about the yellow color. Both of these are examples of "habituation." This is what happens when one of our senses is stimulated again and again. After awhile, you don't notice or react to it anymore, unless it is extreme.

Can caterpillars habituate too? Test your hornworm, or another caterpillar. Dangle a thread so that it gently touches the front half of your caterpillar. Stop after just one or two seconds. How does the caterpillar react? Wait ten seconds or so and do it again. How does the caterpillar react the second time? Wait for ten seconds again and do it a third time. Does the caterpillar still react?

Does the caterpillar react in the same way to a tickle on the back half of his body as he does to a tickle on the front half? Compare the hornworm's reaction to that of a different type of caterpillar. Does the hornworm use his horn when threatened?

Do caterpillars react to a gentle poke with a sharp pencil in the same way they react to a tickle?

THE "RIGHT" REFLEX

Most animals have a position that's more comfortable for them than other postures. Usually this position is with the belly toward the ground and the back upward. If an animal with such a preference is forced to lie on its back, it will usually try to turn itself back over. This urge to "right" itself is often a reflex, just as jerking your hand away from a hot stove is a reflex. (A "reflex" is a response that is automatic. You don't decide to jerk your hand away from a hot burner, you just do it automatically.)

Caterpillars are among those animals that will automatically try to right themselves after being flipped onto their backs. Is there any way you can stop them from trying to do it?

Try this: flip a caterpillar over, and then lay a small stick along his legs so he can hold it. Does this stop his struggling? Do you think the contact between a solid object and his legs sends a message to his brain that he has righted himself, although he hasn't really? How long will holding a stick delay his efforts to right himself?

Section Four

PREDATORS THAT HELP CONTROL THE HARMFUL PLANT-EATERS

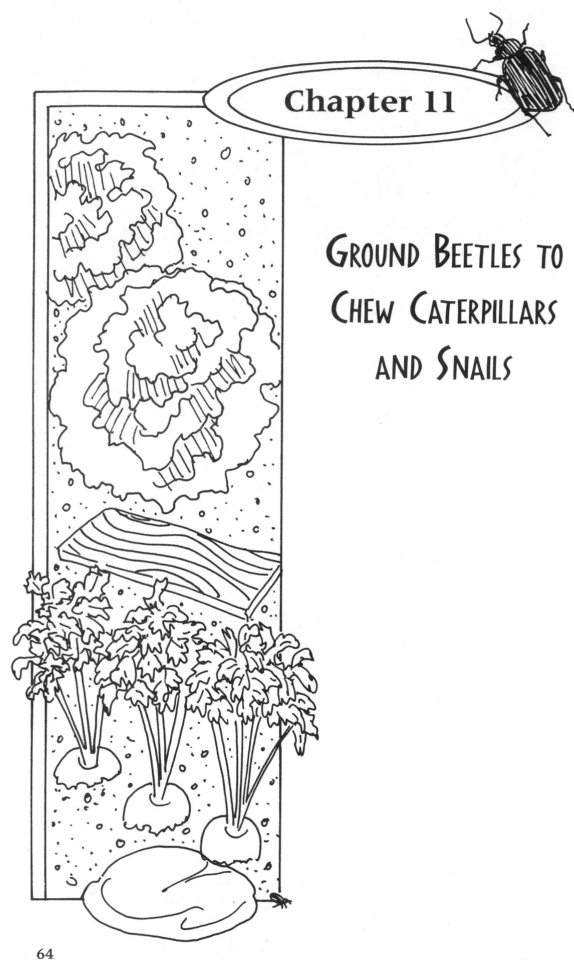

Chapter 11

GROUND BEETLES TO CHEW CATERPILLARS AND SNAILS

Ground beetle is the name of a fierce garden friend that hides under rocks and logs during the day. How can you tell a ground beetle, or carabid beetle, from the many other kinds of beetles? They are usually black, 1/2 to 1 inch long, and have longer legs than most of their relatives. Along the length of their hard front wings are parallel ridges and grooves that not all beetles have. But the way I can tell a ground beetle with one glance is by its behavior when its log is overturned. Many beetles either fly or have a clumsy lumbering walk. But ground beetles dash about, changing directions and rushing madly as if in a panic. And they don't fly. But their ground speed makes them very hard to catch.

WHAT MAKES A BEETLE A BEETLE?

Nearly one-third of all the animal species on earth are beetles! (That's 300 thousand of the approximately one million animal species.) This makes beetles by far the most diverse and successful order of living things.

A beetle is a member of the insect order Coleoptera, which means "sheath wing." This name refers to the front wings of beetles, which are always hard or leathery. These front wings are not actually used for flying but serve as covers for the back wings when the beetle is not flying. The back wings are delicate and clear and are used for flight. The front wings cover the whole rear section of the body (the abdomen) and meet in a straight line down the middle. When the beetle gets ready to fly, the wing covers flip up and forward like the trunk lid of a car. Then the back wings have room to move.

A GROUND BEETLE DINNER

Ground beetles are a gardener's friend because they come out at night to feed on ground-dwelling pests such as caterpillars, small slugs, and snails. They may even climb trees or plants in search of prey. Like spiders, some ground beetles inject their prey with poisons to liquefy the insides. Others tear the prey into small pieces before eating it. A few ground beetle species can spew an irritating liquid from their hind ends to protect themselves (so wear gloves if you handle them).

When I was a biology student, a fellow student of mine kept a small salamander in a damp terrarium with a ground beetle. To his surprise, one of them ate the other. Who do you think ate whom? Surely the salamander (an animal with a backbone) ate the beetle (an insect). Right? No, the ground beetle ate the salamander! Only the tail was left of the unfortunate salamander.

HOW TO ATTRACT GROUND BEETLES

To attract ground beetles to your garden, you can place stones and logs near plants most likely to be bothered by slugs and snails.

If you lift your logs in search of slugs and snails and you find ground beetles, allow them to flee. When you replace the log, they will return in their own time.

TEST THE GROUND BEETLE'S FOOD FAVORITES

Put a ground beetle in a gallon container or larger, with some slightly damp, smooth, flattened soil on the floor. Provide a piece of bark on the soil for cover. Add a small slug or caterpillar. Cover the container opening with a piece of cloth, secured with a rubber band. Place the jar in a dark place and check it at intervals. The beetle may need a day or two to get busy with her jaws. Will she let you watch?

A FIELD EXPERIMENT

Try transferring all of the ground beetles you find to one log. (Release them beside the log—NEVER roll the log onto them or you might crush them.) Keep track of the number of slugs, snails, and insects you find under that log and the other logs. Does the log with more beetles have more or fewer slugs and larvae? What did you predict?

THE PREDATOR VERSUS HERBIVORE RACE

Can you think of predators, besides the ground beetle, that can run fast? Why do most predators need to be quick? The very fastest flier (the falcon), the very fastest runner (the cheetah), and the very fastest swimmer (the sailfish) are all predators. Can you think of predators that don't rely on speed? One is mentioned right in this chapter. What does it use instead of speed to catch its prey?

Find a beetle that is an herbivore (a plant-eater), such as a mealworm beetle, or a Japanese beetle, or a June beetle. (Most beetles are herbivores.) Have a race to see who's fastest, the herbivore or your predatory ground beetle. Using a garbage can lid or a big cooking pot lid, draw a big circle on a piece of poster paper or construction paper. This big circle is your finish line. Make a starting circle right in the middle, the size of a milk jug lid. Place in the starting circle your two beetles. You can keep them both in the right place with an upside-down cup until you're ready. Release them at the same time. Who crosses the big, outer circle first? Who wins? Whom did you predict?

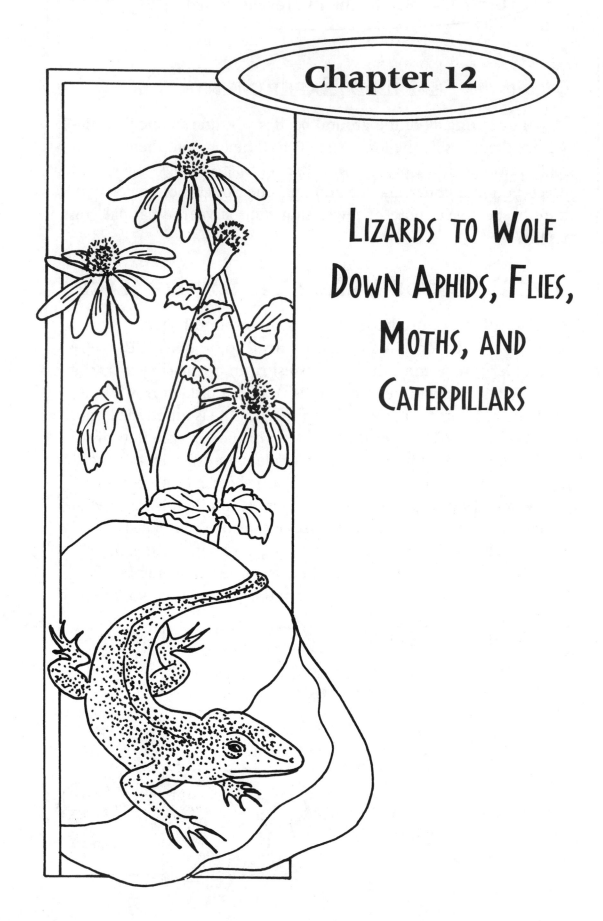

Chapter 12

Lizards to Wolf Down Aphids, Flies, Moths, and Caterpillars

A lizard in your garden may be your favorite guest. Unlike slugs and worms and beetles that stay under logs during the day, lizards enjoy the sunshine. They may climb logs or woodpiles, your pea or cherry tomato stakes, or your trellises in search of warmth or prey. If you move very slowly, you can often watch them quite closely. Some lizards are acrobats—leaping to reach a fly or hanging from a stick by one foot. What fun to watch!

LIZARDS ARE REPTILES

How is a lizard different from an insect? First of all, a lizard is a vertebrate—an animal with a backbone. An insect has no backbone or other internal bones but is supported by its exoskeleton, an outer hard skin.

There are five groups of vertebrates: fishes, amphibians, reptiles, birds, and mammals. Lizards belong to the group called reptiles. Reptiles have scaly skin and lay eggs with a leathery covering that keeps them from drying out. Both of these traits allow reptiles to live in dry places like deserts. Reptiles were the first vertebrates to evolve the ability to survive for long periods and reproduce away from water. The earlier vertebrates, the fishes and amphibians, were more closely tied to water. Fish, of course, breathe under water. Many amphibians are able to breathe out of water, but like the fishes they have moist skin and eggs that must be laid in water or in damp places.

Being free of a watery environment allowed the reptiles to move into new areas of our planet where vertebrates had never been before. Their numbers increased, and they spread out more and more. New ways of life and new body forms evolved. And so began "The Age of Reptiles," dominated by the large dinosaurs.

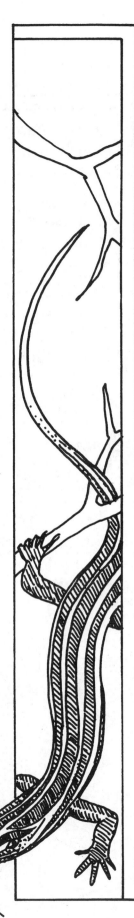

The Age of Reptiles ended with the death of the dinosaurs and the coming of the mammals. The mammals were even more successful than the reptiles. Mammals' ability to generate their own body heat allowed them to invade even more new environments than the dinosaurs had. They were able to survive in very cold places that were off-limits to the cold-blooded reptiles. A cold-blooded animal could not survive on ice. Its body would soon turn to ice too.

Many reptiles still live today, of course. Although none are the size of their extinct cousins, the huge dinosaurs. The reptiles alive today include lizards, snakes, turtles, and crocodiles.

ENTHUSIASTIC GARDEN HELPERS

Lizards will eat all sorts of pesky creatures in the garden, from tiny aphids to big moths that they can barely cram between their jaws. The movement of the prey is what attracts a lizard's attention. So an insect that spends a lot of time sitting still, like a grasshopper, is not as likely to be eaten as an active caterpillar or a scrabbling cricket or a clumsy fly. Lizards do have teeth, but still they swallow their prey whole. If the insect's legs are too long and stick out of the lizard's mouth, the lizard wipes her mouth on a branch to break off the excess leg length. Then she turns the prey with her tongue for the best fit, and down the hatch it goes.

PUSH-UPS ARE SIGNALS

You may notice a lizard bobbing his head up and down, while doing push-ups with his front legs. What is he doing? Can you guess? His behavior means that another lizard of the same species is close by. Male lizards do most of the bobbing. If he bobs at another male, he's saying, "Go away! This is my space!" He may chase the other male, even wrestle with him. If he bobs at a female, it means he's interested in her as a mate. If she finds him acceptable, she may bob back at him.

See if you can play a trick on a lizard. Put a mirror in an area where you see or have seen a lizard. Does it react to its image in a mirror? (Many will.) If it does react, do you think the lizard is a male or a female?

One lizard that bobs readily at a mirror is the green anole. These lizards are the most common pet-store lizards, as well as being commonly found outdoors in many parts of the United States. The skin color of anoles can change quickly, depending upon their mood. Green skin means the lizard is feeling either calm or warm. If a male anole thinks another male is in his private space, as he may when looking in a mirror, then he often turns dark brown. Not only does his color change, but the skin on his neck and back stands up taller, making him look bigger. Of course, he's bobbing at the same time. He may look peculiar to us, but to another male he probably looks scary.

A dark brown color may mean he's cold. Dark colors absorb more heat, and may help him get warm.

How Warm Is Warm Enough?

When we say that lizards and other reptiles are cold-blooded, what we really mean is that their body temperature depends on the temperature around them. (Their bodies may be warm at times and cool at other times.) Since you are a warm-blooded mammal, your body temperature is always the same (unless you are sick).

Lizards can digest their food better when they are warm, which is why they bask in the sun. Do you think lizards bask as much on warm days as on cool days? Or do you think they automatically bask a set amount of time each day regardless of how cool it is? You can answer this question by writing down the air temperature and the number of minutes spent in the sun each time you see a lizard basking. After you have several observations, see if your lizards basked longer on cooler days.

Wise Guy

Anoles have smart-looking faces. They're different from most reptiles, who never really look at you. You may know that a snake or a turtle sees you because it's running from you or hiding. But even if you pick it up, he never looks directly at you. Why is that? It's because most reptiles can't move their eyes much. Their eyes just look at whatever is in front of them. But anoles have very movable eyeballs, like you do. If you get near an anole, he'll cock his head and look at you right in the face. You can see his eyes moving as he studies you. He looks as though he's checking you out, wondering about you. He looks curious. And that makes him look smart.

Chapter 13

Salamanders to Engulf Aphids, Beetles, Slugs, and Pillbugs

Salamanders are amphibians, so they have moist, smooth skin. They may look soft and harmless, but they are voracious predators that swallow their prey whole. Salamanders will eat anything moving that will fit in their mouths—even other salamanders! In your garden they will eat aphids, ants, slugs, spiders, pillbugs, beetles, and more.

Most salamanders are small enough to fit easily in the palm of your hand. Some species live in water their entire lives. Some just start out in water, as a sort of tadpole. Then they move onto land as adults. Other salamanders live their whole lives on land.

The ones that will help you in your garden are the land dwellers, of course. A couple of likely candidates are the slimy salamander or the red-backed salamander. You can invite them to your garden by making a home for them.

WHAT ARE AMPHIBIANS?

First of all, amphibians are vertebrates. This means they have backbones, along with the fishes, the reptiles, the birds, and the mammals.

The class Amphibia includes the salamanders, frogs, toads, and some odd legless creatures called "caecilians." One thing all amphibians have in common is that their eggs must be laid either in water or in a very damp place. Their eggs have no leathery covering to hold moisture in, like reptiles' eggs do. Nor do they have the hard eggshell that birds' eggs have, which serves the same purpose. Amphibians' eggs are much like fish eggs—like little balls of gelatin. In a dry spot, they shrivel up quickly and die.

Amphibians' bodies are more likely to dry up too. They

75

have no scales as reptiles do. And their skin is often damp, which means that in a dry place they lose water quickly through their skin. So amphibians generally live in damp places, even when they're not laying eggs.

People often confuse salamanders with lizards. In fact, some people refer to salamanders as "spring lizards." The body shape of salamanders and lizards is very similar. But their skin is very different. Lizards are reptiles and have dry scaly skin. The two are found in different places too. Salamanders spend their days in damp places—under logs or in streams or other bodies of water. Lizards are out and about in bright sunshine and seldom seek water. With these two clues, you can tell which one you've found.

MAKING A SALAMANDER HOME

A damp rotting log will make a comfortable home in your garden for a woodland salamander. Your little predator will be most useful in controlling pests if you place the log near the vegetables, where most of your pests will be. Before you place your log in the garden, use your hand to make a shallow trough for the log in the soil. Nooks and crevices in the trough will provide spaces under the log for salamanders.

The log home may be shared by the ground beetles of Chapter 11, as well as centipedes, millipedes, crickets, pillbugs, slugs, and snails. Centipedes, with dozens of long legs, can run just as fast as ground beetles. And they're also predators, so they may be helpful in the garden. The millipedes, pillbugs, and crickets may munch somewhat on your garden plants, so if your predators eat them, that's good. But these three are more likely to eat dead plant matter than to attack live plants. So they're not much of a nuisance.

When you look under the log, be sure to replace it in the same position so you won't destroy anyone's home. If you want to release a salamander under a log, leave the log in place and put the salamander next to it. She will find her way under it. Putting the log on top of the salamander may crush her.

An untilled area covered with mulch can also provide cover for salamanders and other predators.

FLASHLIGHT HUNTING FOR SALAMANDERS

Most salamanders that live on land are nocturnal. This means that they hide during the day and wander around looking for food at night. The darkness helps protect them from birds and snakes and raccoons that might eat them while they're out and about. Even mantises can eat them.

If you look after nightfall with a flashlight, you may see salamanders foraging in your garden. You are more likely to see them if you live near a stream or boggy area. Check not only the ground but the leaves of your garden plants. Many salamanders climb at night, searching plants for prey.

Keep a tally at night of how many sightings you make on plants, how many on the ground. You may notice a pattern. Do they climb more often after rains, on damp nights? Why might they do that?

Chapter 14

TOADS TO SWALLOW
CRICKETS, SLUGS,
PILLBUGS, MOTHS,
AND FLIES

Toads are most often seen hopping about on summer evenings. Being predators, they may come at night to an outdoor light that attracts insects. Gardeners sometimes move toads into the garden to eat the slugs and pillbugs and caterpillars that pester the vegetables. A toad will be more likely to stay in your garden if you have made her a home—a cool refuge from the sun and from cats and dogs. An upside-down flowerpot with a door (or propped up on one side) in a shady, damp spot is a good toad home. Toads will occasionally dunk themselves, so a nearby puddle is nice but not absolutely necessary if the whole area is damp. To make use of the toad's pest-eating habits, place the flowerpot home near lettuce, tomatoes, and other plants you want to protect from pests.

MORE DINNER!

You may need to add to the toad's diet to keep her from wandering. Bring her slugs, earthworms, caterpillars, pillbugs, and crickets. You may be able to teach the toad to take creatures from your hand if you are very patient. They are not very fussy. One toad I had in a terrarium ate another smaller toad! Swallowed her whole!

To feed a toad, gently hold a cricket by its back legs, or an earthworm or slug in your palm. Get down low so you look small to the toad. Hold the creature at ground level, where the toad can see it, about a foot away. If she seems interested and does not move away, put your hand a little closer. If you are very still, the toad may lean forward, unfurl her tongue, and nab the wiggling lunch from your hand. Some toads are more easily frightened than others. You'll have to experiment

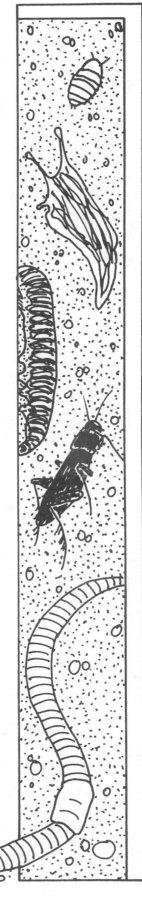

with your own visitor. If you are able to feed her successfully, she will come to expect a tidbit when she sees your outstretched hand and may hop right to it. If the toad seems too frightened to take the bug from your hand, start out by putting the bug or worm on the ground between you and the toad. Toads can learn and remember, so if you want her to trust you, don't ever grab or startle her.

THE "TOADLY" BODY

Notice how a toad will sometimes lean forward to reach his prey, often with one back leg stretched out behind, perhaps for balance. Try leaning forward on your hands and knees. Do you need to stretch a leg behind you too?

Does a toad have a neck? Not really. So do you think he can turn his head? Put a wiggly bug off to the side of a toad, at least a foot away. Does the toad turn his head just a bit to look at it?

Does a toad have ears? He has no outer ears like yours. But he does have ears—round, flat circles on the side of his head. The lumps behind his head are poison glands that protect him somewhat from dogs and cats and other predators. Any animal that eats a toad will probably feel sick afterwards and is unlikely to ever eat another.

HOW ARE TOADS DIFFERENT FROM FROGS AND LIZARDS?

How do you tell a toad from a frog? Frogs usually live in water and have smooth, wet skin. Toads usually live on land and have drier warty skin. But even though a toad feels dry, he still needs moisture in his environment. A lizard has scales to keep him from losing water through his skin. But a toad has no such protection.

Chapter 15

MANTISES TO MINCE ANYTHING THAT MOVES

You may have mantises in your garden a long time before you see them. They are very well camouflaged, green or brown, with twiggy-looking legs and leafy-looking wings. They are easier to spot when they venture onto a wall or car or post where their camouflage fails them. A mantis will eat anything that moves quickly enough to catch its attention, including large wasps and other mantises. They don't swallow their prey whole, as salamanders, toads, and lizards do. Instead, mantises eat their victims bite by bite. Like the talons of an eagle or falcon, the sharp spines on the front legs of a mantis pierce the prey and hold it still while the mantis bites and chews.

GET CLOSE TO OBSERVE

In spite of their ruthless eating habits, mantises are very easy to approach. If you move slowly, you can get as close as you like. A male may fly, but a female won't fly or hide, relying on her camouflage to protect her. Notice how a mantis will turn her head and gaze right at your face, just as an anole will. It makes her look smart too, as if she's studying you. Her spiky arms are folded as if in prayer. A big fat belly means she's full of eggs. How many legs does a mantis have? See her big tummy swell and then deflate just as your chest does when you're breathing. Like other insects, mantises breathe through holes along the sides of the abdomen.

PREDATORS THAT AMBUSH THEIR PREY

Mantises are ambush-style predators, just as web-building spiders are. They sit and wait

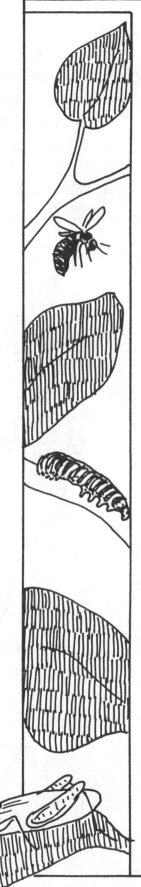

for prey to come to them, hidden by their camouflage. Some predators are "stalkers," like wolves, sharks, or hawks. They move about, searching for prey, instead of sitting still.

Just how still do mantises sit? The next time you spot a mantis, note the time and watch her for several minutes without disturbing her. How many minutes pass before she moves? Do the same thing with a spider in its web. Which stayed still longer?

SHARP-SIGHTED OR NOT?

How well do you think a mantis can see? Predict how close you think a mantis must be to notice movement. Then slowly approach one from the side and see how close you get before she turns her head to look at you. Or bring a cricket to offer a mantis. Move the cricket closer and closer, gently holding its back legs, until you notice the predator moving her head to watch it. How close did you get? Do the test again. Are the results consistent?

Which of your garden pests do mantises like best? Crickets, grasshoppers, caterpillars, sow bugs, pillbugs, slugs, or any other critters you find in the garden? Do the slugs move fast enough to attract their attention? Does the hard shell of a rolled-up pillbug discourage the mantis's bites?

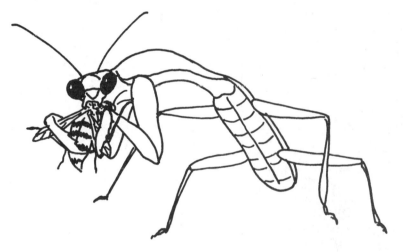

LOOK WHAT I'M HOLDING!

If you want to move your mantis from one area in the garden to another, put the back of your gloved hand in front of her so that she has to step up to get on it. (Mantises would rather walk uphill than down.) Carry her with your hand high so she won't walk up your arm. When you arrive at the desired spot, put your hand a little below the destination and the mantis will step up and off. Your friends will be impressed!

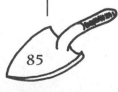

Chapter 16

CRAB SPIDERS TO DRAIN ANY INSECTS

These spiders are named for crabs because their legs are held out at the sides like those of crabs. They can also scuttle sideways quickly, as crabs can.

Crab spiders do not make webs but hunt for prey on the ground, on rocks, and on plants. Their flattened bodies allow them to fit easily into cracks and crevices. Most are shades of brown to blend in with their backgrounds.

Some crab spiders lurk in yellow or white flowers, waiting for any insect that stumbles onto the flower. These particular crab spiders are sometimes called flower spiders. Females are larger than males, with body sizes up to 1/2 inch long. The flower spiders' own color matches that of the flower! So you may not see the predator until she's right in your face. She hopes that her prey will not see her either. She waits in ambush, striking the head or thorax of surprised victims. The flower spider's toxin is powerful enough to kill prey much larger than herself.

ARE SPIDERS INSECTS?

Spiders are closely related to insects. Like insects, spiders are in the phylum Arthropoda. This phylum includes animals with a hard exoskeleton and jointed legs. Other members besides spiders and insects are centipedes, millipedes, and crustaceans.

What's the difference between spiders and insects? The easiest thing to remember is the number of legs—six for insects and eight for spiders. The number of main body sections is different too. Insects have three: the head, thorax, and abdomen. In spiders, the head and thorax have joined to become one part, called the "cephalothorax" (which means head thorax). So spiders have only two main body parts: the cephalothorax and the abdomen.

All spiders have the same mouthparts and feeding habits. All have two fangs that inject poison into the prey and two short structures by the mouth, called "pedi-palps," for holding onto prey. All spiders are predators.

Insects, by contrast, have lots of different feeding habits and a variety of mouthparts. Just in this book we have the stabbing sucking aphids and the stabbing suck-ing assassin bugs, but one is a plant-eater and one is a predator! Then we've got beetles and caterpillars with chomping jaws. And butterflies and flies with soft slurping mouth-parts. Insects have a much broader variety of lifestyles than do spiders.

CAN CRAB SPIDERS CHANGE COLOR?

White crab spiders are usually found on white flowers. Likewise, yellow crab spiders are found on yellow flowers. What happens if you put a white crab spider on a yellow flower? She will slowly change color! The change takes about five or six days. What if you put her on an artificial yellow resting place, such as a yel-low paper circle? That should work too, but you'll have to confine her to keep her there.

Wrong Color!

What if you put a white or yellow crab spider on a red or pink or orange flower? Try it and see. Being unable to match these colors, she will probably leave. (Don't pick up spi-ders with your bare hands, some will bite. You can shake her gently into a cup to move her.)

Does Camouflage Really Help Catch Prey?

Try this experiment to see if camouflage helps. Get some dark brown or black dried peas or beans from your parents. Now choose six white or yellow nectar flowers in your garden that you've seen insects visiting—bees, butterflies, or hover flies. Put a dark pea or bean in three of these nectar flowers positioned in such a way that insects can see it. In the other three, place a white or yellow pea or bean (the same color as the flower). Or simply leave these three flowers with no pea.

Now watch the flowers and record how many insects visit those with the dark peas and how many visit those with camouflaged peas or no peas. Is there a difference?

(Some research has shown that flying insects avoid flowers with small dark objects.)

Chapter 17

Worm Snakes to Eat Soft-Bodied Insects

A worm snake looks very much like an earthworm, with its plain brown back and pink belly. At 7 to 12 inches, it's one of our smallest snakes. The head is small and pointed, and the tail has a sharp but harmless spine.

Worm snakes not only look like worms but are good burrowers and often live in garden soil or under logs and mulch, just as earthworms do. And guess what their favorite food is. You got it—earthworms! They also eat soft-bodied insects, which earns them a spot in this part of the book.

So why does an animal that eats worms look like an earthworm too? Is it to trick the worms? Like a hunter disguised as a deer? That's a good guess. The only problem with that idea is that earthworms are almost blind. They can see light but no shapes or colors. So why do worm snakes look like worms? Try this experiment on your friends and see.

THE WORM SNAKE COLOR EXPERIMENT

Get one sheet of brown construction paper and three sheets of other very different colors, such as white, red, and blue. Cut ten curvy strips from each sheet, about 1/3 or 1/2 inch wide and 7 or 8 inches long. The brown strips represent worm snakes. The other strips are imaginary snake colors. Scatter all the strips over bare soil or leaf mulch in your garden. Have a friend or a parent pretend to be a hungry bird and collect as many strips as they can in eight seconds. Use a longer or shorter time period if necessary. Before you start, make a prediction. Which color do you think will be collected most? Which color will be collected, or captured, least? Were your predictions right?

Do you think a hungry bird or raccoon would be more likely to overlook a brown snake than a brightly colored snake? Maybe worm snakes are colored like earthworms simply because brown, or pinkish brown, is a successful camouflage color for any animal that lives in soil.

HANDLING A WORM SNAKE

Worm snakes don't bite. Check with parents before picking one up, to be sure your identification is right. Some snakes do bite. When handled, a worm snake will squeeze musk from a small opening on its underside called the vent. Musk smells awful. If you were a raccoon, the musk might make you think twice about eating the little worm snake. Some worm snakes will pry between your fingers with the pointy head and the pointy tail, looking for cover. The cool body feels nice wrapped around warm fingers. When you put the snake down, he will burrow quickly into the loose garden soil, out of sight in the blink of an eye.

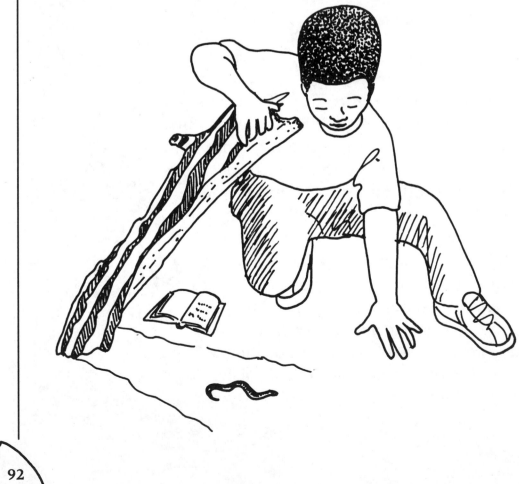

HOME AGAIN, HOME AGAIN

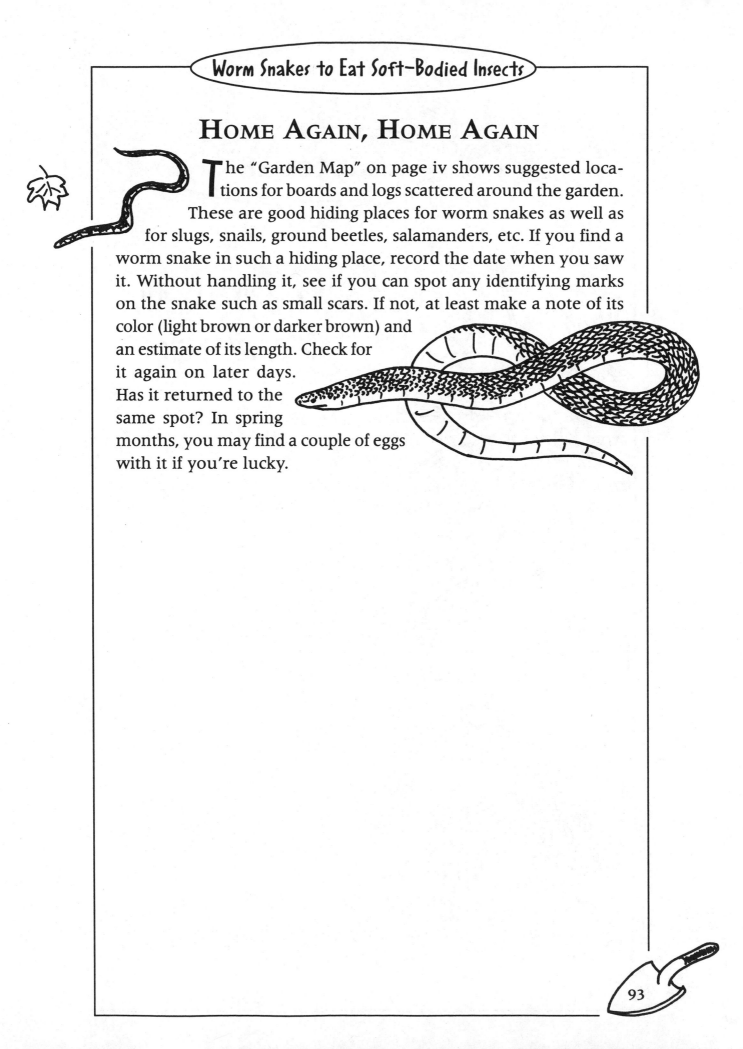

The "Garden Map" on page iv shows suggested locations for boards and logs scattered around the garden. These are good hiding places for worm snakes as well as for slugs, snails, ground beetles, salamanders, etc. If you find a worm snake in such a hiding place, record the date when you saw it. Without handling it, see if you can spot any identifying marks on the snake such as small scars. If not, at least make a note of its color (light brown or darker brown) and an estimate of its length. Check for it again on later days. Has it returned to the same spot? In spring months, you may find a couple of eggs with it if you're lucky.

Chapter 18

Box Turtles to Pulverize Slugs

Box turtles may be attracted to your garden by their taste for strawberries, tomatoes, and cantaloupe. Or they may be in search of a slimy meal of slugs or earthworms. All are highly regarded items on the box turtle menu.

You can tell a box turtle from other turtles by the high domelike shell, which is rather like a box compared to the flatter shells of most turtles. Flat shells are useful in moving through water easily, and most North American turtles live in water. But box turtles live on land. They may soak in shallow water occasionally in hot or dry weather but do not normally swim.

Box turtles can also be identified by the presence of a hinge on the bottom shell or plastron. The hinge works just like the hinge on a door. The box turtle's hinge allows the front of the bottom shell to move upward for a tight fit against the upper shell, or carapace. This completely encloses and protects the turtle's head and front legs when he's frightened, which he probably will be when he sees you. The only other North American turtle with a hinge is Blanding's turtle in the Great Lakes area. Blanding's turtle has a flatter shell and lacks the hooklike beak of the box turtle.

There are several species of box turtles, which have different shell patterns and different locations. The shell of the eastern box turtle has a brown or black background with yellow or orange blotches. There may be a slight ridge down the back. The carapace of the ornate box turtle is brown or black with yellow lines leading away from the center, like rays of a sun.

Unlike the eastern, the ornate box turtle has a flat or dipped-in area on top of the carapace. The Florida box turtle has a pattern similar to that of the ornate but with fewer lines or rays. The three-toed box turtle may have a faint pattern similar to that of the ornate or may be almost plain brown.

Male eastern box turtles usually have red eyes. Females have brown or yellow eyes.

DON'T SLAM THAT DOOR!

Some box turtles are shyer than others. I've met some that stayed shut up in their shells so long I fell asleep waiting. These very shy ones may slam shut again every time you move. But I've met others so bold that they wouldn't close the shell even when I picked them up.

If a turtle reacts to you by sealing herself in, record the amount of time that passes before she comes out again. If you're lucky enough to see her again another day, repeat this procedure. Is she less afraid of you in later encounters? What do you predict?

Okay Slam It! But at Least Tell Me WHY!

What factors cause a box turtle to withdraw into its shell? One of its five senses (sight, hearing, smell, taste, or touch) is sending a message to its brain that something strange is going on around it. We know that the sight of something odd can make a box turtle withdraw. We know that being touched or lifted can make it shut the shell tight. But what about its other senses? Can a strange sound alone make a turtle close its shell? You can test this by sneaking up behind a turtle and saying something sharply or blowing a whistle.

Many ground-dwellers are sensitive to vibrations. How could you test whether box turtles are? Can you stamp the ground quietly so that he can feel it but not hear it or see it?

What about smell? Can a turtle be alarmed through his sense of smell alone? If you've found a turtle that is no longer afraid of your hand, you can test this idea. Get two cotton swabs. Dip one in water and one in a mixture of water and ammonia. Hold the cotton swab with water under the turtle's head, briefly, not touching its skin. Then repeat this procedure with the cotton swab dipped in ammonia and water. BE VERY CAREFUL NOT TO TOUCH HIS SKIN OR EYES WITH AMMONIA. Ammonia has a strong odor. Did he react by withdrawing into his shell?

Why did we use one cotton swab with water only? This tells us whether the turtle is reacting to the smell of the ammonia or the sight of the wet cotton swab.

Is Your Turtle Visitor a Vegetarian or a Predator?

What'll it be—salad or steak? Individual turtles have different favorites. One turtle I knew turned up her nose at anything other than strawberries. Another preferred earthworms. Both ignored the tomatoes and cantaloupe that many box turtles enjoy. Of course, if they visit your garden, you hope they're after the irksome slugs. And most box turtles do like slugs.

What good entertainment it is to watch one go down the hatch! First the turtle's head and neck will come way out of her shell as she peers down at the slug. Then (if it's a big slug) she'll bite it in two, with the sharp edge of her toothless jaw, and swallow half without chewing. The next half of the slug, having oozed a bit while the turtle swallowed the first half, will leave a froth of slug slime all around her mouth as she snarfs it. When the turtle has finished the slug, she is unable to tidy herself. Having no mirror or napkin, she remains a mess. But she doesn't seem to care.

If you have a turtle visitor, test her to see what she prefers. Offer a slug and a strawberry, or a slug and a tomato chunk. Or a slug and a small wad of earthworms. Keep a record of her choices and see if she is consistent in her preferences.

Can You Keep a Turtle Away from the Tomatoes and Cantaloupes?

Bites taken in random spots on your tomatoes may be the work of a turtle. How can you keep them away? Keeping your tomatoes off the ground is the best protection against turtles. Tying the plants to stakes will get most of the tomatoes out of reach.

Will a Turtle Eat from Your Hand?

I have not tried feeding box turtles by hand, but I think it can be done. I know that box turtles are smart enough to learn and that they lose their fear with familiarity. If offering a slug or other goody from your hand, you should wear a heavy glove or place the morsel on a piece of cardboard—something to keep your fingers from being bitten. That beaklike jaw could do some damage.

Chapter 19

Assassin Bugs to Drain Pesky Bugs

The assassin bug is a murderer of insects. He helps out in the garden by killing pests like Japanese beetles and caterpillars. The assassin bug's weapon is a long needlelike beak on the end of a long thin head. The oddly shaped head of an assassin bug is a good identifying feature. The needlelike beak swivels up against his "chest" when not in use or down and out when ready to make a puncture.

Most kinds of assassin bugs are only about 1/2 inch long. But they vary. One kind is about 1 1/4 inch—the "wheel bug." He's called this because of the curved hump along the midline of his thorax, with a line of teeth along the top of it. He looks like part of a cogwheel is glued to the middle of his back.

Many assassin bugs have front legs that are specially equipped for grasping prey—more muscular and having a row of spikes. However, the wheel bug doesn't. Its front legs look just like its other four legs. But they do a fine job of grasping prey anyway.

FEED AN ASSASSIN BUG

Assassin bugs hang out on leafy plants waiting for prey. You can feed one if you move slowly. If he is a small one, offer a small pillbug. If he is a wheel bug, put a beetle or a caterpillar in front of him. He'll approach at a slow, lumbering pace, seize it with his two front legs, and stab it with his beak. The beetle will struggle, legs flailing, but there's no escape. The flailing slows as the assassin bug injects strong digestive juices into the beetle to liquefy its insides. Then he sucks out the resulting fluid, taking an hour or more. He may poke around inside the prey, just as you poke around

with a straw, searching for the last drop in a cup. When he's finished, the beetle is filled only with air, like a Rice Krispie. Hold it up to the light, and you can see the light through it.

You might want to offer the assassin bug water in a spoon or on a leaf. If he's thirsty, he'll suck it up through his beak, as an elephant does with its trunk.

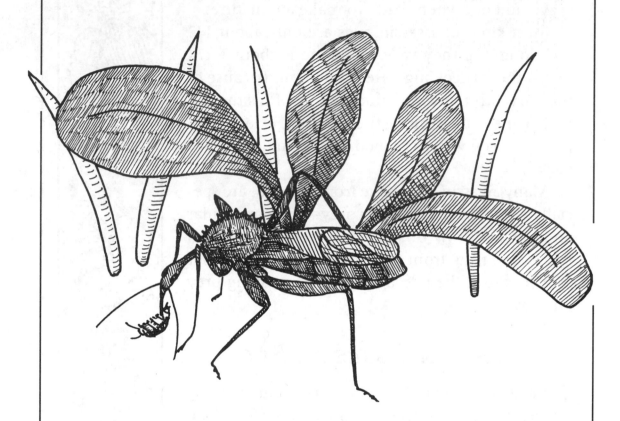

MAKE AN ASSASSIN BUG PUPPET

If you have a dark sock with a hole in the toe and a flexible drinking straw, you can make an assassin bug puppet. Put the sock over your hand and mark about where the eyes should be. Then glue two dark circles or fluffy balls on the sock for eyes. While the sock is on your hand, put the end of the straw through the hole in the sock. The bendable end of the straw should be closest to your hand so you can bend the straw back against your puppet's chest when it's not in use. Use the drawing to help you position your hand, the sock, and the straw to look like a real assassin bug.

When he's hungry, your assassin bug model can move his beak into piercing position. Then, all stuffed animals in your house had better beware! Assassin bug is on the prowl!

TRUE BUGS

Assassin bugs belong to the order of "true bugs," the Hemiptera. Many other insects are commonly called bugs (ladybugs, spittle bugs, lightning bugs, June bugs, etc.), but they are not true bugs because they are not hemipterans. Insects in this group all have piercing beaks, and all have wings that are clear in part and leathery in part. The true bugs are, to me, the most interesting order of insects because many of them are fearsome predators that will eat readily while you watch. It will give you the willies to watch. Many are aquatic, like the giant water bug. This is the predatory insect in Annie Dillard's *Pilgrim at Tinker Creek* that deflates a frog in front of her eyes. Giant water bugs can even kill and eat snakes. The ones I've had in aquaria eat crickets, tadpoles, small fish, and each other!

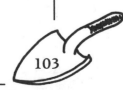

Chapter 20

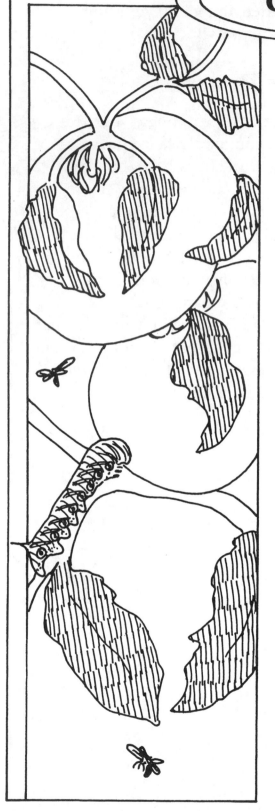

Braconid Wasps to Liquefy Hornworms

Most of us are afraid of wasps. But if you were a hornworm caterpillar, you'd really have reason to be afraid of wasps. The tiny braconid wasp lays its eggs inside the body of the hornworm. If you saw the movie *Alien*, you may remember the crablike alien that laid its eggs inside the astronaut, with unpleasant results for the astronaut. The results are equally unpleasant for the caterpillar. When the wasp eggs hatch, the wormlike wasp larvae eat the insides of the living caterpillar! But the caterpillar keeps on truckin', chomping big holes in your tomatoes and tomato leaves—for awhile. The hornworm gets slower and slower as more and more of its internal organs are munched by the wasp larvae. When the wasp larvae are grown and ready to turn into adult wasps, they burrow up through the skin of the hornworm and make little cocoons on the outside of the caterpillar's body. The cocoons, stuck on the hornworm's back and sides, look like bunches of tiny rice grains on end. After a few days, tiny wasps, no bigger than gnats, emerge from the cocoons. The hornworm dies, and the wasps move on to mate and lay eggs in new hornworms.

As yucky as this sounds, the wasps are a great help to gardeners. A single hornworm, up to 4 inches long, can do a lot of damage to a tomato plant, pepper plant, or eggplant.

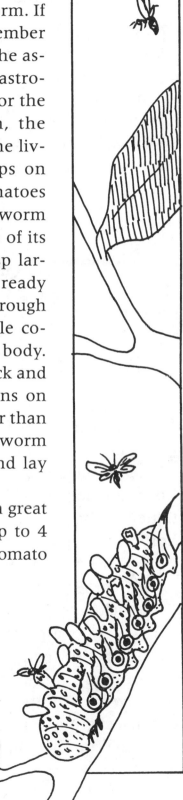

How Do the Wasp Eggs Get Inside the Hornworm?

The female wasp, like many female insects, has a long pointed ovipositor (egg depositor) on the tip of her abdomen. With the tip of her ovipositor she injects the eggs just under the skin of the hornworm. (For the hornworm, it's rather like getting a shot.) At first the larvae may feed on just the body juices of the hornworm so the caterpillar can continue to live. If the hornworm dies before the wasp larvae are grown, the larvae are out of luck.

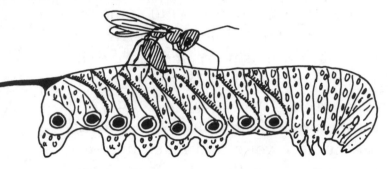

What Exactly Is a Braconid Wasp?

A braconid wasp is in the wasp family Braconidae, which is only one of many wasp families. They are black or brown and smaller than most wasps, only 1/10 to 1/2 inch long. The adult wasps eat nectar from flowers. They will be attracted to your garden by small flowers with lots of nectar, like alyssum (which is mentioned in Chapter 3). Not all species of braconids lay their eggs in hornworms, but most are parasites of some insect. Each braconid species has its own special insect victim. And there's another family of small wasps that parasitize insects—the ichneumon wasps.

All wasps are in the insect order Hymenoptera, which includes also bees, ants, and termites.

There are not a lot of parasitic insects. Most parasites are roundworms, flatworms, mites, or members of some other noninsect group. The braconids and ichneumons together make up the majority of parasitic insects.

106

WHO EATS THE MOST?

This is an experiment to tell you how braconid wasp parasites affect the hornworms' appetite. Plant one tomato plant in each of two pots. When the plants are about a foot tall, put some hornworms with cocoons on one tomato plant and hornworms without cocoons on the other. (The one without cocoons may have wasp larvae inside, but even so, it shouldn't be as damaged as the one with cocoons.) Keep track for a couple of days of how many tomato leaves are eaten on each plant. Are the hornworms with wasp cocoons slower? Do they eat at all?

HORNWORM RACES

Use a checkerboard or chessboard to compare the movement of hornworms with and without wasp cocoons. Test several caterpillars, one at a time. Place the hornworm in a corner of the board and gently prod it from the rear. How many squares on the board does it cross in a one-minute period? Which ones cross more squares, the ones with cocoons or the ones without cocoons?

PARASITIZE YOUR STUFFED ANIMALS!

A parasite is an animal, such as a flea, tick, or tapeworm, or braconid wasp, that feeds off another animal without killing it. At least, not right away. A parasitized animal is one that has been attacked by parasites. If your dog or cat has fleas, ticks, or intestinal worms, then it has been parasitized. If you've ever had head lice or pinworms, then you have been parasitized! Some parasites of course are more harmful than others. The ones we and our pets get are more pesky than dangerous.

Here's how you can make a stuffed animal appear to be covered by wasp cocoons, or parasitized. The end of a cotton swab looks very much like a braconid wasp cocoon, only bigger. But it's about the right size for a stuffed animal. Cut the ends off several cotton swabs. If you can pull the cotton ends off the swabs without cutting the sticks, that's even better. Glue the tip of each cotton oval onto the surface of the animal so that the oval stands up straight. The glue probably won't come off so be careful which animal you choose. Explain to your friends or your teacher how the real parasite works.

If you don't want to sacrifice a stuffed animal, glue the "cocoons" on a drawing of a caterpillar (or your big sister!) instead.

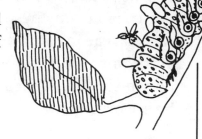

Decomposers Recycle the Dead Plants

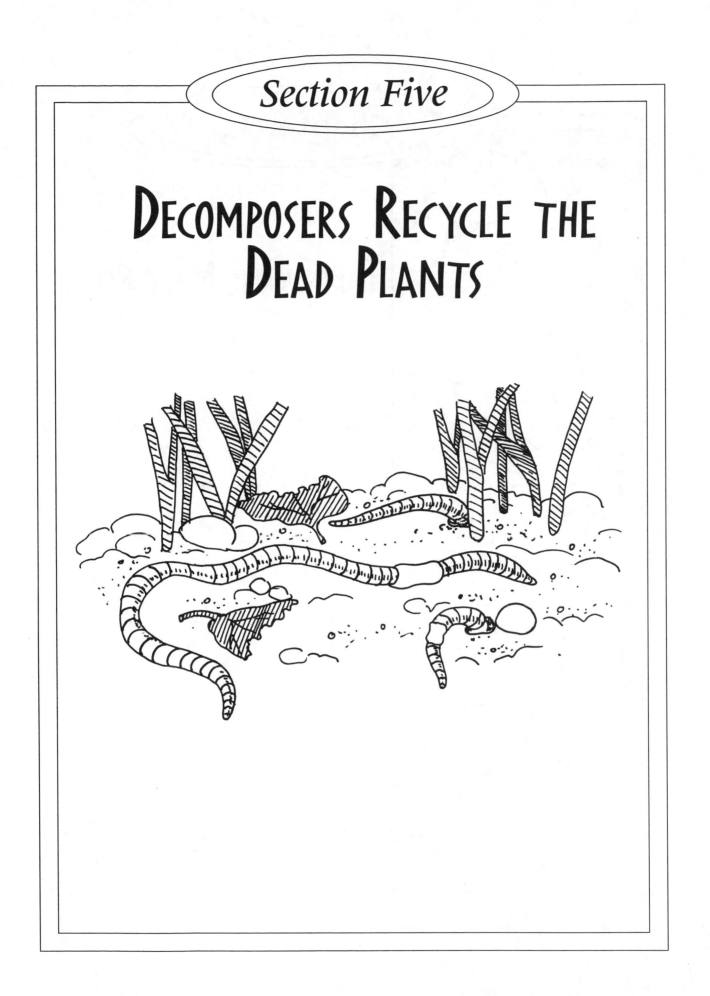

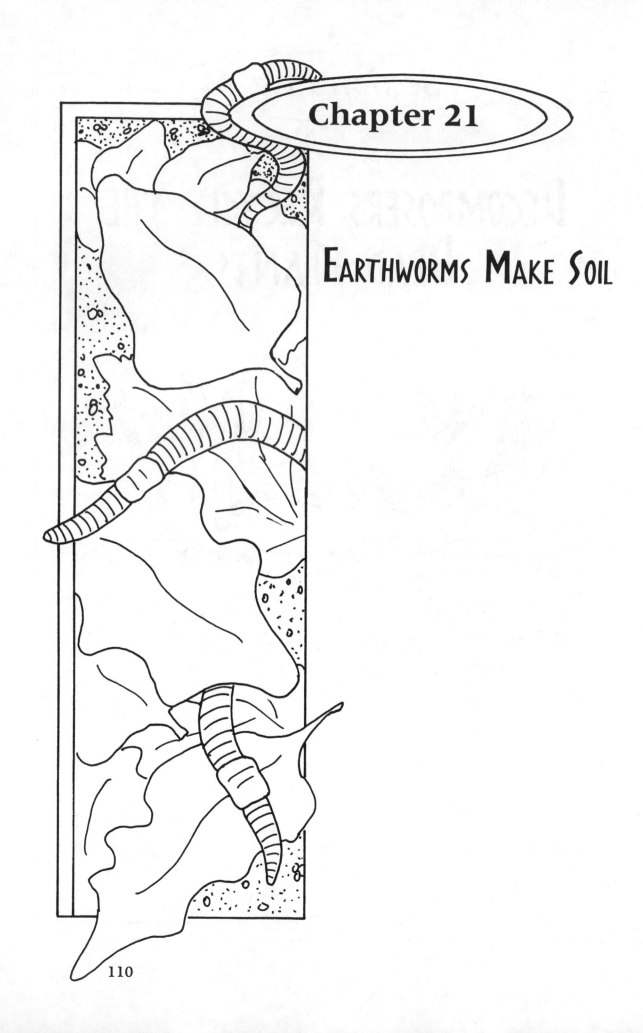

Chapter 21

EARTHWORMS MAKE SOIL

110

The Jobs in Nature We've Already Learned

You've already met the plants, who can magically take the energy in sunlight and transfer it into food that all living things depend upon. Then we met the aphids and the caterpillars and the snails and slugs, who eat plants just as we do and sometimes compete with us for it. We saw that the butterflies, hover flies, and birds eat plant parts too, without damaging the plant. Then we met the predators, who eat the plant-eaters. Predators help control the numbers of plant-eaters. We humans are predators as well as plant-eaters, aren't we?

One More Job

Plants, plant-eaters, predators—isn't that all the jobs there are in nature? What else is left? What about someone to clean up the mess? Nature's custodians! What happens to dead plants and animal parts that no one has eaten? One answer is that bacteria and fungi attack them and break them down into tiny pieces that become part of the soil again. But there are also animals who help break them down. Living things who have this job are called "decomposers." Earthworms are decomposers. They eat dead leaves, grind them up inside their bodies and pass them out again as very rich soil—our very best soil. Earthworms are probably more important than any other single animal for creating new good soil.

LOOK AT IT SQUISH ITSELF UP

Look at an earthworm crawl across a table top. It does not move in an S-shaped curve as a snake does, or in a loop as an inchworm does, or with tiny steps as a caterpillar does. An earthworm moves by compressing its body like an accordion and then stretching it out again. Rather like one of those metal coils made to look like a snake that you cram into a can as a gag. Or like a Slinky. The worm has muscles that run around its body like a lot of belts, and they squeeze its insides, forcing its body to grow longer and thinner. It has other muscles that run the length of its body, like a lot of very long neckties. When these muscles contract, they force its body to become shorter and thicker. These two different kinds of muscles take turns. To move the worm forward, the circling muscles squeeze its front half out long, onto new ground. When the head end comes to a stop, tiny bristles anchor it to the ground. Then those long muscles contract and shorten, pulling the tail end up closer to the head. And so the worm makes progress. You can easily see the work these two types of muscles do if you watch a worm creeping along. Lie on the floor and see if you can do it. No bending at the waist allowed! We don't have the circling muscles or the long muscles. Even if we did, our skeleton would keep us from changing our length.

What Is That Collar?

The collarlike band around the earthworm's body is called the "clitellum." It's useful in making the worm's egg sac. The head end of a worm is the end closest to the clitellum.

A WORM HOTEL

A compost pile is an excellent place to keep worms. You can pile dead leaves into a space between a shed and a fence or in a corner of a fence, or you can just pile them on the ground if you've a space where the wind won't scatter them. Perhaps an adult will help you build a compost compartment. It needs three or four walls but no top or bottom. At least some of the walls must have large spaces for air to pass through. Hose the leaf pile down occasionally so the leaves stay damp. Worms aren't keen on oak leaves—provide other types of leaves as well. When the leaves on the bottom are partly decayed (and damp), your pile will be a suitable worm home.

You can keep a miniature worm hotel indoors. Fill a clear glass or plastic terrarium halfway with damp dark brown garden soil. Put a few earthworms in and cover it with cloth, secured to the terrarium with a rubber band. The worms will come out at night, looking for food. Offer broken dead leaves (not oak), chopped celery leaves, coffee grounds, and tiny bits of vegetables (very small amounts). What do they like best? After a few days or weeks of this, you'll be able to see new areas of dark soil in your container. The earthworm made it and it's called "castings." It looks rather like the sand that dribbles from your fingers when you make a drip castle but very dark brown.

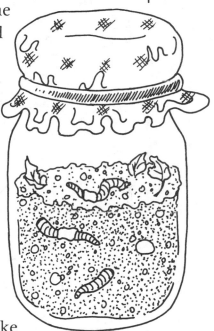

RED LIGHT!

If you see an earthworm exploring your garden after dark, briefly shine a flashlight on its "head" (the end closest to the worm's "collar"). How does it react? Try to find some red cellophane or a red filter for your flashlight. Does the worm reach the same way to red light as to white light?

WORM CAMPING

Make a little tent for your worm by folding a small square of black paper in half. Place it over your worm so it looks like the two slanted sides of a roof. Let one end of the worm stick out. Now shine a flashlight on it from above. Does the earthworm pull its head in? If its tail end is sticking out instead, does it pull that end in as quickly? Light on its tail is usually less annoying to the worm than light on its head.

Section Six

WRAPPING IT UP

Chapter 22

What Happens to the Plants and Animals When Cold Weather Comes?

Harvesting lettuce in November? Yes, it's possible. Some people replant cool-weather vegetables like lettuce, carrots, onions, and radishes in late summer. Their growth will slow down as it gets cooler, but you will probably be able to keep harvesting these vegetables until the first frost. (The first frost is the first night that the temperature goes below freezing.) In fact, if you cover them with a sheet of plastic or a bedsheet on nights when the temperature dips below 32°F, your leafy vegetables (like lettuce) may last even longer.

But most of your garden plants will die when the first frost comes. When that happens, remove them from the garden. Any plants that were healthy up until then can go on the compost pile. Any that were diseased or infested with pests should not go on the compost. Pests and plant diseases from the compost pile that are hiding in your new soil can reinfect next year's garden.

Cover your bare garden with a heavy layer of mulch, or with black plastic for the winter, to keep weeds from growing during warm spells.

Adult insects usually die when it gets cold. For most insect species, only one of the life stages is adapted to surviving in cold weather. Often it is the egg or pupa stage that overwinters. Insects don't eat during either of these stages, and food may be scarce in winter.

For aphids, mantises, and spiders, it is the eggs that are able to survive the winter. The eggs hatch in spring and the life cycle starts over.

For butterfly and moth species, the pupa is usually the life stage designed to survive in winter. Encased in a chrysalis skin or cocoon, sometimes under a log, it's somewhat protected from cold temperatures and ice. The adult emerges in spring, ready to mate and lay eggs.

Many beetle species overwinter as larvae. They may burrow down into the soil, which protects

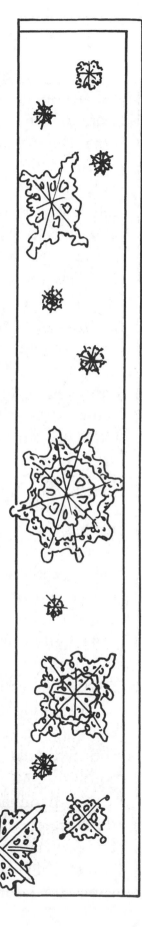

them from ice and freezing temperatures. If you have any beetle species in your garden that are a problem, like Japanese beetles, you may want to turn your soil every few weeks in winter and leave it uncovered. This exposes the beetle larvae in the soil to insect-eating birds.

Amphibians and reptiles often hibernate in winter. To hibernate, an animal finds a refuge for the winter where it goes into a long sleep. In this hibernation sleep, the animal doesn't eat or do any of its usual functions (except breathing) for months. You may come across hibernating snakes or turtles or toads in winter. You may find them under logs or burrowed deep into soil or mud. They may seem very sluggish. Leave them where you found them. Leaving them exposed may kill them.

If you see a reptile or amphibian out and about in winter, you can be sure it knows what it's doing. Some reptiles, like anoles, can tolerate mild to medium winters without hibernating. They may sun themselves for warmth on a cool sunny day.

Many birds fly south for winter, but lots stay behind too. The American goldfinch (in Chapter 6) can be found all winter in most of the United States. If you decide to feed seed-eating birds in winter by setting out a feeder, be sure to keep it up all winter. Birds that come to feeders become dependent on the feeders. If the feeder becomes empty during a cold period, even for a day, the birds may die. Finches, chickadees, titmice, cardinals, and grosbeaks are all seed-eaters that come willingly to feeders. The growing number of feeders in the United States has caused some birds to change their migration habits! Some birds that used to fly south for winter now stay behind and depend upon feeders to get them through snowy months.

Hummingbirds are basically tropical birds. They spend only summers in the United States, except for a couple of species in the southwestern corner of the United States. The other hummers fly south into Mexico and farther for winter.

So ... animals are set to take care of themselves in winter. They don't need help (unless they become dependent on bird feeders) and probably do better without it. On their own, they'll be back in summer. Plant their favorite flowers, set up those habitats, grow some lunch for them, and they'll be back!

INDEX

INDEX OF ACTIVITIES (BY TITLE)